GODDESSES & O

YEVONDE: A PORTRAIT

KATE SALWAY

BALCONY BOOKS
1990

First published in 1990 by
Balcony Books, 19 Westbourne Road,
London N7 8AN.

© Kate Salway, 1990

All rights reserved

ISBN 1 86 9846 10 9

Design and Production
by Stuart Hamilton and Gail Tandy

Typesetting by William Chapple

Printed in Great Britain

Thanks are due to the following for their help:

Kathy Biggar, Maurice Broomfield, Ron Callender, Lawrence N. Hole, Rosina Muriel Oliver, Terence Pepper, Chloë Scott.
Margaret Biggart, Tessa Codrington, Susan Hoyle, Paula Shaw (assistants of the 1950s and 1960s)
Myrtle Oxland Symmonds (solarization printer)
Samuel B. King (Vivex printer)
Mike Leibling of Saatchi and Saatchi
Sarah Woodcock of The Theatre Museum
David Doughan of The Fawcett Library
A.C. Cooper and Wimbledon Photographic
Lady George Scott, Professor Margaret Harker, Hugo Vickers, Peter Espé, Keith de Lellis, David Dawson, C.K. Chiu, Judy Goldhill, Ian Wolseley, Miranda Spicer, literary agent Xandra Hardie, and especially, John Searle.

Picture Credits

Cover and p. 60: Royal Photographic Society; Frontispiece and pp. 31, 52, 55, 57, 59, 60, 61: Yevonde Portrait Archive; pp. 3 & 5: Mary Evans/The Fawcett Library; p. 11: Imperial War Museum; p. 25: Theatre Museum/V&A; pp. 20 & 21: National Motor Museum; p. 21: Sport and General; pp 40, 60 & 64: National Portrait Gallery; p.28: Ronald Callender; p. 33: Chiu; p. 47: Kathy Biggar; pp. 51 & 55: Maurice Broomfield; p. 31: Greater London Photography Library; pp. 20 & 23: Royal Maritime Museum; *Medusa*: Private Collection, London; pp. 41 & 46: Private Collection, London; pp. 63 & 68: Keith de Lellis, New York; p. 23: B.F.I. stills; pp 24, 39, 42: I.L.N.

While every effort has been made to contact copyright owners, the author and publishers regret that this has not always been possible.

Contents

Foreword and Preface

Acknowledgements and Introduction

Chapter I
Suffrage versus Glamour   1893–1914 1

An Edwardian education; A teenage Suffragette;
Apprenticeship with Lallie Charles.

Chapter II
First Studio, First War   1914–1918 9

Setting up in 1914; Outbreak of War;
War work on the land; Back to Photography.

Chapter III
Second Cowman to Society Photographer   1918–1932 15

Marriage to a Playwright; Daytona Beach;
with Bluebird and cousin Malcolm; Charlie Chaplin.

Chapter IV
Fortune Smiles   1932–1936 27

Colour portraits with Vivex; Berkeley Square;
Society weddings; The Queen Mary for *Fortune*;
First colour exhibition; Lectures in Paris.

Chapter V
Goddesses and Others   1935–1946 43

Goddesses in Vivex; Widowhood; War again;
Firewatching, country life and breakfasts at the Ritz.

Chapter VI
Doves and Predators   1946–1975 53

Homes and Gardens; A Knightsbridge studio;
Solarized portraits; Ethiopia;
Distinguished Women;
Life's work at the R.P.S.

Bibliography, Exhibition List and Index 70

Foreword
Mrs Middleton, by Kathleen M. Biggar A.R.P.S.

At last! With enormous devotion and enthusiasm Kate Salway has produced and published an account of Madame Yevonde's life and work. As someone who has admired and loved Mrs Middleton dearly I know she would have enjoyed and approved of this book. She would have relished the dedication with which the author has done her research and the perseverance she has shown in publishing. I am convinced that Mrs Middleton would have liked and respected the author.

Yevonde Middleton's remarkable passion for photography was matched only by her love of people, which together produced an uncanny ability to portray something special in all her subjects. Her talent to capture her sitters at the right moment, her ability to relate to people of all ages from all walks of life and her knowing inquisitive eye, that could see beyond a physical appearance, remained with her until the day she died.

Between 1914 and 1974 over ten thousand sitters came to her studios. Her most innovative years were the 1930s when she launched her business into colour. Although the onset of war and the death of her husband in 1939 were a watershed in her life, illustrated by her remarkable still life "Crisis" which she gave to me in 1973, Madame Yevonde continued to run her photographic business until the year before she died. Her enthusiasm never waned and she has left behind a formidable collection of portraits from over sixty years.

This book is the result of Kate Salway's fascination with and admiration for this very special lady. I commend it to you.

Mrs Middleton by Kathy Biggar, 1973.

Preface
by Ron Callender F.I.I.P., F.R.P.S.

It was something of a mystery to understand why Mrs Middleton of Campden Hill captured the hearts of so many people and was able to exert so much influence – until you met her. My own personal files on the lady are 14 centimetres thick and cover an 80th birthday celebration at The Royal Photographic Society, London, an account of an unusual colour process which she exploited to good advantage in the 1930s, and my personal tribute to her published in *The British Journal of Photography* in 1988.

It is not unreasonable to claim a "Madame Yevonde Industry" which began in 1921 when she delivered "the most witty and progressive lecture to the Congress of the Professional Photographers Association, and was urged to be the first lady member of Council. The plea was declined; Mrs Middleton had other matters to occupy her alert mind.

Her output of photography was remarkable by any standard and through her concentration in the 'Vivex' colour printing process, she has left a unique record of society between the two world wars. The prints will not fade or discolour – and should outlive the commercially available colour photographs being produced today. There are specimens of photographs on permanent display at the National Museum of Photography, Film and Television; colour originals were featured in the "Chasing Rainbows" exhibition held at the Science Museum in 1982, her work earned a place in "Modern British Photographers 1919–1939" organised by the Arts Council of Great Britain in 1980 and the exhibition "Women Photographers in Britain 1900 – the Present" in 1986.

Around the world, Madame Yevonde's reputation does its bit for British photography. In America, her prints exchange hands for hundreds of dollars; in Finland, a group of photographers respect her work and plan exhibitions of her photographs. In the lounge of the Duke of Buccleuch's Castle is an original print of His Grace as a pageboy in the thirties; in dressing the set for *Brideshead Revisited*, the designer selected a print from the Madame Yevonde collection. There is no need to call a halt to the industry – the industrious Mrs Middleton would have approved.

Acknowledgements

Like Maude Coffin Pratt, the fictional heroine of Paul Theroux's novel *Picture Palace*, Madame Yevonde 'levelled the peepstones of her Third Eye at the beautiful and the obscure'. Though not going as far as *Snake swallowing a pig* or *Eel in a toilet*, she may have felt equally detached at her own retrospective in 1973, when a book about her life's work, or an autobiography should have been published. But Yevonde had cancer and was to die two years later. She willed her negatives and business to Ann Forshaw, at whose untimely death in 1986 Lawrence Hole was left to own and administer the Yevonde Portrait Archive.

In 1981, Terence Pepper of the National Portrait Gallery Photographic Collection had introduced Lawrence Hole, who brought me the set of enormous and heavy leather-bound daybooks dating from 1923 to 1955. Those of 1914 to 1923 and 1930 to 1941 are missing; the latter a tragic gap, for it was Yevonde's most prolific and prestigious period, with vital evidence of both her circle and clients. However, during the 1920s and the 1940s, and judging by her portraits in *The Sketch*, *The Tatler* and *The Bystander* throughout the 1930s, there were as many as four sittings a day, six days a week.

Author and photographer Ron Callender, friend of Vivex-inventor, Dr D.A. Spencer, was chief organiser of the 1973 show. He introduced Chloe Scott Norman, Yevonde's niece, who gave me family portraits and stories of her unconventional aunt. Kathy Biggar, Yevonde's assistant and friend of the last ten years of her life gave me in 1981 the unpublished memoir-notes left to her. All three also gave constant encouragement and support. Professor Margaret Harker led me to Madame's two business partners – Rosina Muriel Oliver, now 94, and professional photographer Maurice Broomfield, who were with Yevonde 1920–1945 and 1946–1952 respectively.

In 1982, Dame Rebecca West, though ill and confined to bed, reminisced with great enthusiasm about her 'dear friend Madame Yevonde'. Drawerfuls of photographs of herself by Yevonde between 1924 and 1968 were produced, the most memorable being those with her young son Anthony West and their huge old English sheepdog. Arthur Koestler corresponded concerning his own portraits, especially that taken in 1955 with his black labrador Attila at Long Barn, his sixteenth century farmhouse in Kent. In Bloomsbury, artist and beauty Oriel Ross, Countess Poulett, talked of posing for Yevonde in 1926 and of her lovely sister-in-law Lady Bridget Poulett, who is the nereid Arethusa in the Goddesses of 1935.

At the same time Dr David Mellor suggested to me the idea that a book on Madame Yevonde might be written as *Testament of Youth*; it did feel important that her personality should predominate and that it would not be a critique (already ably done by Val Williams and David Mellor, see bibliography). This approach precluded publication by the N.P.G., who after reading my manuscript last year decided to publish their own book on Yevonde. Their subsequent text is a document-based account. But my intent was to paint the ship and not just the barnacles, for, unlike Maude Coffin Pratt, Madame Yevonde did have a life as well as her photography.

Kate Salway 1990

Introduction

> 'Technical efficiency is a commonplace in our modern world, but the man who will use his imagination is a rare creature'
> Mme Yevonde, address to the R.P.S., *Why Colour?* December 1932.

Madame Yevonde is one of the most intriguing of British photographers. Not just for her pioneering of colour and her imaginative fantasy-portraits, but also for the ten thousand black and white portraits, chiefly of celebrities between 1914 and 1973 and, not least, her extraordinary personality. She was vivacious, knowing, energetic, sharp and critical, whilst full of the wisecracks that made her so popular. Paradoxically, she adored glamour and glamorous women whilst remaining a feminist; she mixed with Society and voted Labour. All who knew her say the same thing, that she was a complete original.

Her contribution to photography was as an enterprising initiator for colour prints for which she had to fight continually. 'I always felt that criticism about colour photography being unnatural was bunk' she declared, 'and even though the process is still in its infancy, it opens up a new world to the photographer.' Inspired by her motto 'Be original or die' her colour photographs were daringly different. She used photographic colour in ways not seen before – red on red, sensually, symbolically, to create atmosphere, promote feelings, convey moods. She found it exciting, some found it vulgar.

The first person to exhibit colour portrait photographs in this country in 1932, she used colour filters over her lens and lights with the British Vivex Colour process. She produced portraits which fulfilled the sitter's reasons for coming to her studio, and portraits with the addition of imaginative ideas for herself. Few photographers had yet applied an artist's imagination to their work; those portraitists of *Blitz* and *The Face* of the last decade owe something to her style.

It was not an early affinity with pictorial imagery, the camera or the photograph which led towards her career, Yevonde took up the profession out of a strong desire for personal independence. 'I wanted to earn money of my own' she states. Two world wars, which she refers to as the Kaiser's and Hitler's respectively, early widowhood and the closing of Vivex Colour Printing obstructed her life and career; but she persisted, leaving behind a considerable archive of the faces of sixty years. This book outlines the absurd and romantic events of her life that led to the creation of that joyous legacy.

Self-Portrait, 1917.

I
Suffrage versus Glamour, 1893 – 1914

Born in Streatham on January 5th 1893 she was christened Yevonde Philone, and no-one believed it was her real name. When she was nine, she asked her father Frederick Cumbers, a manufacturer of printing inks, what made the sky blue. He explained that the sky wasn't really blue, that colour was an illusion produced by a combination of rays which split up into factions to become the blue of the sky, the green of the grass and the red of the geranium. Later, at his office in Farringdon Street, she saw huge barrels filled with brightly coloured inks. "You can't still say there's no such thing as colour" she said, and he laughed and took from his drawer three pictures of an Egyptian slave-girl on shiny transparent paper, one yellow, one red and one blue. He put the three on top of each other which showed the girl in her natural colouring. Yevonde felt he had performed a miracle which she never forgot.

All her earliest memories are of colourful scenes, especially the blazing turbans and flashing jewels of Indian princes on white horses in the procession for Queen Victoria's Jubilee of 1898 seen from the window of her uncle's shop in the Strand. This uncle, William Campbell, was the father of Malcolm Campbell, then a schoolboy, later the racing driver.

The Cumbers family were happy and prosperous, moving house from Streatham to Bromley when Yevonde was six. She and her younger sister Verena spent their early childhood in a felicitous round of parties, charades, the theatre and fancy dress balls, surrounded by their dormice, lizards, doves, pigeons, canaries and dachshund, Fagg. Their parents were loving, kind and supportive, hiring to educate them a series of governesses, whom Yevonde declared to be 'complete idiots'. Ethel, her mother, always chose the applicant with the worst hard-luck story; easily bored, Yevonde despised their attempts at instruction, eventually becoming so difficult that at fourteen she was sent away to boarding-school.

Lingholt, at Hindhead in Surrey in 1907, was a very modern and progressive school in attitude (though it still had earth closets). Its motto, 'Freely we serve because we freely love' (an odd choice for a girls' school) was carved over the sideboard in the dining-room, leading new girls to believe it referred to the number of helpings allowed. The headmistress, Miss Moir, was well-liked and respected. Competitiveness was not encouraged, no prizes or form-places, and the pupils were not worked hard. It was believed that the young required their strength for building their bodies and their brains would be all the keener for not being overstressed. Miss Moir did not presume to educate, she felt she opened doors for children to go through and educate themselves. Yevonde thrived in this atmosphere, and was popular. She was tall with huge brown eyes and one long dark plait down her back: the humour, energy and liveliness which characterised her later personality were already apparent.

In 1939 she recalled, 'Lingholt was the first school to start Scouting for Girls. Loveday Hext (a wild child from Cornwall, thin as a lath with large grey eyes) and Dorothea Molesworth (whose passion was collecting beetles) were responsible. They

1
GODDESSES
& OTHERS

formed a patrol called the Night Hawks of which I became a member. The idea caught on like wildfire and there were soon two other patrols. Lighting a fire with not more than three matches in a wind, tracking and cooking over a camp-fire etc., we had terrific inter-patrol warfare, stealing each other's kit, compasses, jackknives, pencils, tracking-irons; inventing such blood-thirsty games with battles in which girls were bashed on the head with staves, clothes torn and real injuries sustained that Miss Moir had to intervene and the Night Hawks became Guides under the supervision of the games mistress'.

When she was sixteen, she and Rena were sent to a convent school at Verviers in Belgium for a year. Hopelessly bored again, she turned inward, her thoughts concerned with liberty and freedom, particularly that of women. It was then that she became a suffragette, officially joining the movement the following year, in 1910. Yevonde begged her parents to send her to Paris, to the Guilde Internationale attached to the Sorbonne. Here she was scolded for writing an essay on Mary Wollstonecraft as her favourite heroine, and for being a suffragette which, she was told, should be left for the disillusioned and disappointed. Disgusted with this, she spent most of her time trekking round obscure corners of Paris trying to persuade members of the various French suffrage societies to join the huge international demonstration to be held in London that summer.

Yevonde had followed the course of the suffragette movement since the formation of the Women's Social and Political Union in Manchester in 1904. The next year, Christabel Pankhurst and Annie Kenney, by their imprisonment, managed to break the press silence on votes for women. In 1906 the Pankhursts moved to London setting up an office in Clements Inn from where they published 'Votes for Women'. The years 1907 to 1909 saw increasingly large demonstrations followed by hunger strikes of many of those arrested and forcible feeding. In 1911 Prime Minister Asquith declared, 'I am head of the government, and I am not going to make myself responsible for the introduction of a measure which I do not believe to be in the best interests of the country'.

At seventeen, Yevonde came home to Bromley. The six months that followed were spent in the routine of the majority of respectable suburban girls of the time – the theatre, shopping, flower-arranging, gossip, tepid female tennis, cycling up and down the High Street, coffee and doughnuts at Munder's. In short, pottering and waiting for marriage left her bored and unhappy. In deciding she must be independent, would not marry and must earn her own living, she was torn, for she wanted most of all to devote herself full-time to the suffragette cause. But this would not support her and would almost certainly lead to imprisonment of which she was terrified. She feared the harassment of militant suffragettes, forcible feeding, and the 'cat and mouse' tactic of releasing hunger-striking women at the point of death, then re-arresting them when restored to health. She wrote 'I would gladly have embarked on a career of wickedness and violence to obtain political freedom, but I was frightened. The leaders of the W.S.P.U. conducted the campaign of violence like a war, to destroy property but not endanger life. If you signed on, you signed on for the lot. You couldn't say, I don't mind smashing windows but I draw the line at setting fire to a church. I could not face prison

3
GODDESSES
& OTHERS

Above left: *Yevonde's portrait of her father Frederick Cumbers, 1914.*

Above right: *Studio beach: Yevonde standing, and Verena, 1900.*

Right: *A suffragette selling 'The Suffragette' circa 1913.*

and forcible feeding. I must get a career – that is the only way to help the cause'. So she sold 'The Suffragette' on street-corners (chiefly outside the Criterion at Piccadilly Circus), marched in processions, chalked pavements and wore a sandwich-board to advertise meetings, some of which she arranged at her home.

At one, she held forth on venereal disease and child assault to an assortment of startled and embarrassed girls her own age, with no converts. Undaunted, she organised another with two militant suffragettes as speakers – Evelyn Sharp and Evelyn Greene – both of whom had suffered imprisonment. This was a great success; she felt, 'they were sympathetic, brave and charming women; I longed to be even a little like them.'

Yevonde spent much time thinking about her future. The prospect of marriage and producing daughters like herself did not appeal. 'What was the alternative–' she wrote, 'I might take a lover, and go to the bad. But mother would be so frightfully upset.' So at seventeen she decided to cut out love and marriage from her life and earn her own living. She considered and rejected the following:

'(a) Being a doctor: Exams too difficult. Training too expensive though rather fancied myself as the "healing physician".

(b) Being an Architect: Exams too difficult.

(c) Being a Farmer: Very interested. Hankered after wide open spaces. Family hostile.

(d) Being an Author: Had an itch to write. Didn't know how to set about it.

(e) Being an Actress: Ditto. Ditto.
Wasn't particularly stage-struck but had written and acted in plays since the age of seven.

(f) Being a Hospital Nurse: Not sufficiently self-sacrificing. Hated the thought of bed-pans, night-duty and smells.

(g) Devoting myself to the Suffragette cause: Tempting. Would not solve economic problem.'

One day, she writes, 'after a rather stodgy lunch of cold mutton, boiled potatoes and treacle pudding, I was flopping in a hard, shiny leather chair in the dining room reading *The Suffragette*. I was skimming the advertisements when I saw one from a photographer who required a pupil'. This was Lena Connell, in St. John's Wood, and next day Yevonde went for an interview. The Connell studio at 50 Grove End Road was too far for her to travel from Bromley every day – but she had seen enough to make a decision. She would become a photographer, and study with someone good, who was also a woman.

The most popular photographer of the day was Lallie Charles; the magazines and newspapers were full of her charming, soft and slightly over-exposed sepia bromides, chiefly of women. 'She was a terrific slap-up success', Yevonde wrote; who lost no time in contacting her, going to 39a Curzon Street, Mayfair, for an interview. Lallie Charles was about forty at the time and at the height of her success. Everything in her studio and

Lena Connell, self-portrait, 1910.   *Lady Ramsay, by Lallie Charles, 1912.*

5
GODDESSES
& OTHERS

house was pink, even her photographs had a soft pink tinge. She charged between five and thirty guineas for a sitting. For props she used a lattice window, Chippendale chairs, Empire furniture, silk roses and lilies and a bearskin rug, and always a light background, then vignetting the print. A butler and a maid were employed especially to help people change. Some women brought three or four corsets and would spend the whole morning dressing and undressing for photographs. The female sitters were transformed into submissive young girls. Lallie Charles let her pekinese Chang decide whether Yevonde should be her pupil: he snuffled at her ankles and wagged his tail. There was a premium of thirty guineas, tuition would last three years, with the premium paid back in wages of five shillings a week the first year, ten shillings the second and fifteen the third.

Yevonde's mother and father were sympathetic and pleased. Happy at having taken the first step towards independence, she felt 'frightfully important' rushing off to catch the 8.35 a.m. to town every morning. At the studio she was soon able to quickly load dark slides into the camera, number negatives, index the sittings book, answer the phone, interview the unimportant clients and take Chang for walks in Green Park. (In the neighbourhood she was known as 'Cleopatra' because of her haughty manner and the way she did her hair). Here she didn't learn so much about photography as about running a business and the world of sophisticated people.

In her apple-green overall Yevonde would take the silk roses and lilies from tissue-lined boxes and arrange them in blue Chinese vases, then drape pink chiffon over pedestals and pink velvet chairs. The printing, spotting, retouching, mounting and despatching of the photographs was done at a large house in Regent's Park known as 'The Works'. Only the developing was done at Curzon Street, by Yevonde and two girls rocking dishes of exposed plates in developer – which had to be rocked gently and evenly by the glow of a dim red safelight. Her fingers soon became stained brown, of which she was immensely proud. At parties Yevonde would wave her hands about in an affected manner and say, "It's the chemicals you know, I'm a photographer."

After a year, she asked to go to 'The Works'. Here the successful negatives were first given to the retoucher who cut away double chins, over-prominent busts, and thick ankles, with a knife. After rubbing the negative with a solution known as 'medium', wrinkles and blemishes were removed with a pencil. This took skill, as a likeness had to be retained. The negative was then printed, trimmed and mounted and sent to the finisher who softened lines and retouching marks with paint-brush and watercolours, knife, gum, chalks and pumice powder, and who gave sitters long curling eyelashes and soft curving mouths. The little white spots on the print caused by flecks of dust, had to be spotted-in to match the sepia-pink colours of the print. This was Yevonde's first task; the delicate surface of Lallie Charles' glossy printing paper (which was matted by squeezing it whilst wet onto a piece of ground glass) did not take paint easily, and the soft pink tone was hard to match. Then she learned mounting with a dry-mounting machine, smoothing out the tissues to be attached to the print. She had only just grasped the fundamentals of these techniques when Madame ordered her back to Curzon Street as she had decided to move studios. Business had gone down; no one seemed to want to be photographed by her any more, and the portraits she took were returned with complaints that they faded. There were endless grumbles and resittings. Lallie Charles decided a new studio would solve her problems; she spent extravagantly on herself and on alterations to the new house and studio further down Curzon Street. She held a lavish opening to which no-one came. The photographs taken at the new studio were hopeless. With creditors pressing, she took the builders to court, lost, and was made a bankrupt. But before the court case, Yevonde left. 'Like a cheerful young rat deserting, I departed, but I felt sorrow, regret and love for the sinking ship'.

Gaby Deslys as Suzette at the Globe Theatre, 1917.

7
GODDESSES
& OTHERS

8
GODDESSES
& OTHERS

Lady Helen Vincent, 1914.

II
First Studio, First War 1914 – 1918

Yevonde had learned from the troubles of Lallie Charles, but had only taken one photograph in her two and a half years there, so in 1914 she decided to teach herself photography by setting up on her own. Her father helped with capital and she found an inexpensive studio at 92 Victoria Street for £100 a year. It had a large, well-lit, north-facing L-shaped room, and was fitted up perfectly as the outgoing tenant was a photographer.

From him she bought a camera and stand with a Dallmeyer portrait lens, a Marion arc lamp for foggy days, printing frames, developing dishes, fixing tanks and Winchesters (bottles holding eighty fluid ounces). In addition she acquired a new dry-mounting machine and a re-touching desk and for props, a spinet from the Caledonian market, a Cromwellian oak bench, and chairs and tables from her friend the poster artist Charles Dawson. The dark-room was little more than a cupboard, with no room for an enlarger, so the photographs were taken on glass plates at the size required. The developing dishes and hypo tanks had to be big enough to hold at least six fifteen by twelve inch plates, so they had to be kept on the floor; proofs on glossy printing-out paper were done on the flat roof outside the studio window. With an anthracite stove that smelt vile and orange curtains up at the windows nothing could be further from Lallie Charles' pink cocoons.

Yevonde realised that the most important requirements for success were to know the job and have plenty of ideas, have the right contacts and work hard. She wrote 'By great good luck I had adopted an art-trade-profession-science that, like myself, was not properly grown up'. But first, specimen photographs were needed to show to prospective clients. Her sister Rena was posed to look like a number of different sitters – hair flowing, hair piled up, evening dress, sports dress, with dog, with cat, rose in mouth, looking sensitive, looking lively. Finally she put up a sign that read 'Madame Yevonde – Portrait Photographer'.

One of the first portraits was a court sitting of the surgeon Swinford Edwards and his wife. At the last minute she remembered there was no red carpet, so the liftman was sent to measure the pavement and rush to the Army and Navy Stores for red felt, which when unrolled was three feet short. The pictures were a success but Yevonde was dissatisfied with her work: it was too like that of Lallie Charles. She worried also that they might fade. So she stopped using bromide paper and printed with a platinotype toned sepia, adopting dark backgrounds and making the quality of the negatives more substantial. The resulting prints were interesting and people liked them. She liked to have her sitters well lit; detesting what she called 'two-tone portraits' she aimed to show the subjects as they were normally seen by friends and relatives, as 'natural' as possible. Through a theatrical agency her portraits began to appear in the weekly papers. She did complementary sittings of celebrated and attractive people (such as Gaby Deslys, Edward VII's mistress) to get her name known.

In June 1914, the leading portraitist in London, E.O. Hoppe came to see Yevonde and explained that he had been watching her work in the papers and would like her to be his partner. She was flattered but preferred to remain independent, for her business had grown and prospered. Hoppe went on to open studios in New York and Berlin.

Yevonde's studio had only been set up for seven months when war broke out. It was an awful blow. She felt she should close down right away and take up war work, but hesitated for it would be a waste of her father's money. As most said the war would be over by Christmas, she decided to wait and see, meanwhile waving goodbye to soldiers marching past her studio on their way to Victoria Station and the front. Young soldiers in khaki did come to be photographed, but, like many middle-class women, Yevonde felt great patriotic fervour and a desire to contribute more to the war effort. The Suffragettes, who, since 1904, had been battling with the government, now became more supportive of the war effort than anyone. On July 17th, 1915, Mrs Emmeline Pankhurst organised a 'right to serve' demonstration of thirty thousand women through London when the government was slow in finding outlets for willing female workers.

Towards the end of 1915 Yevonde's conscience gnawed at her. Her contribution to the war effort, apart from photographing soldiers, their wives and sweethearts, consisted of some indifferent knitting in khaki wool and a great many visits to *Chu Chin Chow* and *A Little Bit of Fluff*. In March 1915 the government began to compile a register of women prepared to do agricultural work, and towards the end of that year posters appeared asking for women to take the place of agricultural labourers. One poster she found compelling showed a woman standing in the middle of a pink field beside a plough, a soldier holding one hand and saying to her "Goodbye, I leave the land to you". The image kept returning to her, so early in the new year she went out and bought her kit –two pairs of hob-nail boots (in which she could hardly walk) a bottle-green corduroy tunic coat and breeches, some holland smocks for milking, leather gaiters, thick jerseys and underclothes. Her family were furious.

She went off feeling miserable. It was snowing and 'the land' was cold and bleak. At the farm in Essex they had to get up at 4 a.m. to walk across fields to another farm to milk cows, walking back for a breakfast of porridge, tongue and bread and treacle. The other women with her were Sylvia Marshall (of Marshall and Snelgrove), Ursula Sichel, daughter of the writer Walter Sichel and other daughters of the well-to-do, moved to contribute to the war effort. She came to be employed as a second cowman at Powerscroft Farm outside Chelmsford, taking the place of a cowman who had joined the Colours the day before. For twelve hours hard work seven days a week, she received fifteen shillings, from which she had to pay back twelve to the farmer for her keep. Her duties were to fetch the cows in from the fields, milk them, then drive the cans in a horse and cart to the station to catch the London train. She could not lift the heavy cans from the cart onto the platform by herself and had to pay a porter to help her. She then cleaned the dairy, walls and floor, scrubbed out the milk pails, fed the calves and the bull, cleaned out the cowshed after which came spreading manure, and hoeing or singling in the fields. In the afternoons she fetched the cows from the fields, milked them again and took them back. One very hot day she had to shear a flock of sheep; the exertion of holding them down made her nose bleed.

Woman Land-worker, 1915.

11
GODDESSES
& OTHERS

During the summer of 1916 whilst spudding thistles alone in a wheatfield she heard a low hum and looking up saw twenty-two enormous planes flying in perfect formation towards London; they were German Gothas. When they reached Romford, one tiny fighter plane flew up into them. Trembling with rage, she heard the daylight raid on London and almost fainted with anger as they all flew back triumphantly.

When she got a day off, her family found her much changed. She had lost over a stone and her face had turned a muddy brown with bags under the eyes. Milking twenty-eight cows a day caused painful cramp which attacked her hands and arms in the night and she was getting no sleep. Her father felt that the farmer was exploiting Yevonde's patriotic fervour and begged her to see a doctor. She was not being properly fed, and after fainting, was found to have anaemia. This brought the war work to an end.

Mrs Wansey Bayly as a Bird of Paradise, 1920.

Yevonde's portrait of her friend the dancer Margaret Morris, 1920.

14
GODDESSES
& OTHERS

April 12, 1922 — The Sketch

The Wife of an Honourable and Gallant Member.

FORMERLY MISS MARY CURZON : VISCOUNTESS CURZON.

Viscountess Curzon is the beautiful wife of Captain Viscount Curzon, M.P. for the South Division of Battersea, son of the Earl of Howe, and was formerly Miss Mary Curzon. She was married in 1907, and has a son, the Hon. Edward Richard Assheton Penn Curzon, born in 1908, and a daughter, the Hon. Georgiana Mary, who is two years younger. The announcement that Lord Curzon, who is a Captain in the Royal Volunteer Naval Reserve, has received the R.N.V.R. Officers' decoration appeared in a recent issue of the "Gazette."

PHOTOGRAPH BY YEVONDE, EXCLUSIVE TO "THE SKETCH."

Viscountess Curzon, 1922.

III
From Second Cowman to Society Photographer 1918–1933

Yevonde returned to her studio to get her business thriving once again. When the newspaper proprietors decided to cut down photographers' reproduction fees she joined the Professional Photographers' Association to protest. Some of the press started their own studios for taking portraits of celebrities, which frightened photographers, fortunately for the independent studios these were not a success. She worked hard to attract large numbers of sitters: major and minor aristocracy; the Winston Churchills, Arnold Bennett, Rebecca West (who immediately became a close friend) Noel Coward, Cathleen Nesbitt, Barbara Cartland and Hermione Baddeley were among those who came for portraits. Serge Lifar and four ballerinas of the Ballets Russes commissioned portraits which Yevonde took at His Majesty's Theatre where they were appearing in Stravinsky's *Apollon Musagete*. Edith Evans' portrait was taken at Wyndham's and that of Martita Hunt at the Globe. Yevonde went to the Savoy to shoot Sinclair Lewis; Sacheverell Sitwell and Aldous Huxley came to the studio. She enjoyed the sessions with Evelyn Waugh who was not photogenic – always looking as though about to explode with anger – but his squashing presence and highly developed practice of making people feel uncomfortable amused her. *The Sketch* had been publishing her portraits since 1917.

The Great War had changed Yevonde's attitude to life, and love, considerably. Towards the end of 1919, through her work she met Edgar Middleton, a journalist, author and promising playwright. She was twenty-six; striking rather than pretty, tall and slim with short, dark, wavy hair, huge brown expressive eyes and long slim legs. Edgar was two years younger, rather shy, sensitive and considered good-looking. They fell in love and after a whirlwind courtship Edgar asked her to marry him: six weeks later they were married at St Clement's Dane in the Strand on Friday February 13th 1920.

During the war, Edgar had served as Second Lieutenant in the Essex Regiment and as a Flight Sub-Lieutenant with the Royal Naval Air Service, holding an Aeronaut's Certificate. He had already published *Aircraft* 1916, *The Way of the Air* 1917, *Airfare* and *Tails Up* 1918, *The Kingdom of the Air* 1919 and *The Great War in the Air* 1920. He contributed to *The Times* and *The Daily Mail* and was the London correspondent for *The New York Sun*.

Incredibly, Yevonde asked Edgar before they were married, if he would like her to give up her work: she wanted to show that she was willing to sacrifice her precious independence for love. To her great relief, Edgar replied that it would be a mistake. But on their honeymoon in Cornwall, not only did she lose her wedding ring in the sea, which Edgar refused to replace, but he told her that he could not bear the idea of having children. This upset Yevonde very much, as marriage without children seemed quite senseless. She thought he might change his mind: instead he became more adamant than ever. Edgar was very ambitious and driven, needing success more than anything;

Edgar Middleton, playwright, by Yevonde, 1927.

16
GODDESSES
& OTHERS

in pursuit of it he was both cynical and selfish. He had no intention of moving from his tiny chambers in the Temple just off Fleet Street, so Yevonde had to move in with him at 3, Dr Johnson's Buildings, overlooking Hare Court.

In 1922, Edgar began to work as sports editor for *The Westminster Gazette* during the day, and during the evening, including Sundays, had determined to make himself a successful playwright. The minute he came home from work – at ten in the evening when the Temple gate was locked – he would start his own writing which went on until midnight, during which she was forbidden to speak a word and scarcely allowed even to move. The tension was almost too much for the sociable, talkative Yevonde. When midnight struck on the huge Law Courts clock he would stop. Yevonde encouraged friends to drop in and gossip over whisky, or they might walk their cats around the lanes and Courts of the Temple, chatting to neighbours. They had many interesting, often eccentric friends – Colonel Jack Ball, who had talked with Hitler; the dancer Margaret Morris; Allen Lane, who started Penguin Books; law lords and society beauties. Very occasionally they would go to the theatre and to films, and at Yevonde's instigation give mad fancy-dress parties with dancing competitions, charades and debates which Edgar loathed – he quite often would order everyone home. As there was no kitchen in the flat, Yevonde did not cook, so they ate out until they finally hired a housekeeper. For

Yevonde, the silent evenings dragged, so she became more involved in her own work.

First she moved to a larger studio at 100 Victoria Street which had two darkrooms so that she could employ her own printer. The premises had a shopwindow on the street in which to display photographs. It faced south, so she shut out the daylight with blinds and used lights, which she had come to feel produced more flattering results. Late in 1920, Muriel Oliver, with whom Yevonde had been at school, came to be her pupil before setting up on her own in Manchester in 1922, as a partner in a company they formed under the name Yevonde. As plays for London were first tried out in Manchester, leading actors and actresses went to the Manchester Yevonde Studio for their portraits for the London production. Muriel also took her camera to the South of France each spring to photograph celebrities and society people for the London magazines.

By April, 1921, the twenty-seven year old Yevonde's fame in London was such that she was the first woman to be asked to lecture to the Congress of the Professional Photographers' Association. Richard Speaight, of one of the most well-known Bond Street studios at the time, gave her great encouragement. She produced what was described in *The British Journal of Photography* as 'certainly the most witty and progressive lecture delivered to Congress'. The subject was 'Photographic Portraiture from a woman's point of view'. To illustrate the lecture she went to see all the professional women photographers working at the time and borrowed slides from them. They were: Lena Connell, Yvonne Gregory, Alice Hughes, Florence Van Damm, Mrs Angus Basil, Dorothy Wilding, Mrs Marion Neilson, Dora Head, Madame Pestel and Madame Genia Reinberg. Muriel Oliver remembers that Yevonde looked absolutely wonderful in a superb Chinese shawl, delivering the lecture with a great sense of theatre.

However, the lecture upset many photographers and for weeks the photographic

Dr Johnson's Buildings overlooking Hare Court in The Temple.

press was filled with indignant letters about her pronouncements:

> 'Women have done much to popularise portrait photography... it would have languished and died but for the interest of women; ... mothers wanting portraits of their sons, daughters – for their fiancés, society beauties every time they buy a new hat, the charming actress who must be photographed often and always. Women seem to possess all the natural gifts essential to a good portraitist... such as personality, patience and intuition. The sitter ought to be the predominating factor in a successful portrait. Men portraitists are apt to forget this; they are inclined to lose the sitter in a maze of technique luxuriating in the cleverness and beauty of their own medium. A pleasant pesonality goes further towards making a successful portrait than a perfect print. The sitter must come first and everything be done to make them as comfortable in the studio as possible, or the odds are very much against a life-like portrait. A women is more likely to create this atmosphere than a man. Her tact and sympathy are acknowledged facts, and she ought to possess in a marked degree the power of putting the sitter at ease... The quickness with which a woman's brain works is an enormous help in dealing with sitters. Scientists tell us that it tires more easily than a man's but it acts spontaneously and with greater rapidity, a tremendous advantage in the studio especially with children and difficult sitters. Our intuition here is of much more value than man's much-prized logic.'

After discussing likeness, retouching, assistants and women portraitists in other countries, she went on,

> 'Women abroad have not taken up portrait photography so extensively as here, with the exception of America. They have not had the opportunity for self-expression and development... which people sometimes forget in judging women's creative work in art. Isolated and exceptional women have always broken through the artificial sex barrier... the dreams and aspirations of the majority of women find no means of direct self-expression at all. Here in England while women have only just been privileged to sit on juries and in Parliament, they have been closely connected with photography, almost since its birth. They have contributed largely to the rearing of and caring for the precious infant – both as assistants and operators. Mrs Cameron, for one, was doing splendid work as far back as the 1860s. She was a brilliant pioneer who photographed nearly all the eminent men and women of her day.'

Then the working methods of individual British photographers such as Alice Hughes and Lallie Charles were outlined before Yevonde went on to list pitfalls...

> 'We must also admit that she has her faults – and she has shown a weakness by falling into the rut of the one idea... a failing all artists are prone to and women more than men. I believe this is due to the fact that we delight too much in keeping

ourselves to ourselves. This has been a great fault of mine in the past . . . it is only since I have come out a little that I realise what an indifferent photographer I am . . . We must see one another's work, criticise, and receive criticism or we shall never improve . . . We must realise perfection is not creation. That although we have won fame by some special style or thought, to repeat ourselves is not only non-creative and purely mechanical but must lead to destruction or deterioration of business. We also realise that she is often untrained, that having attained a certain amount of success she does not bother to improve. She climbs to the top of the tree with not much trouble, and then shows a tendency to recline in comfort, never realising that there are other higher and perhaps more beautiful trees to be tackled and that if she refrains from further climbing, she may find she has been left in the shade.'

Compliments were paid by Marcus Adams, Richard Speaight and Herbert Lambert and Yevonde was presented with a bouquet of blue irises by Mrs Frank Brown, the wife of the President.

Yevonde had some strange assignments whilst at the Victoria Street Studio; one was to photograph a noble lord in his coffin, during which she and her camera nearly fell into the coffin with him. Another she describes,

'Once I photographed a strange lady of title. She was, I suppose, over seventy at the time, short and squat. Her skin under the rouge was the colour of very old ivory and the wrinkles were deeply furrowed, the eyes protruded like those of a toad and the lids hung over them in loose folds. She wore a tam o' shanter perched on her head at a jaunty angle and she had on a green and grey plaid suit and stout country shoes. She was lame, and could not walk unsupported. With her came a good-looking gigolo in a well-cut suit. His lady went into the dressing room to make ready for the photograph and he and I discussed the relative merits of Monte Carlo or Juan les Pins (neither of which I have ever visited) as a summer resort. The dressing room door slowly opened, her ladyship stood leaning on two sticks. She had taken off her blouse, the top of her stays showed above the skirt band and dangling far below her hips were the tops of woollen combinations, which were slipped down and turned back over the corsets. Diamond earrings hung from her old, distended ears, from her dyed red hair a magnificent diamond brooch flashed. The shoulders and breasts were naked except for a piece of transparent tulle which trailed over the skirt and brushed against her stout country shoes. Her enormous breasts, with large purple nipples, hung below her waist like gourds. She smiled with the utmost self-possession and asked if I liked the idea of the jewel in her hair? I stared in silence. The gigolo thought the idea "perfectly charming and very chic". I began the sitting. "I suppose you only want a head?" I said doubtfully, glancing at the extraordinary effect below the waist. "Head and shoulders" she simpered, "I have always been complimented on the whiteness of my neck" and the gigolo said "She has such a lovely shoulder line . . . you mustn't fail to get that".

20
GODDESSES
& OTHERS

Left: *Malcolm Campbell at Daytona Beach, Florida, 1931.*

Above: *There were few passengers on the 'Homeric' in 1931.*

Below: *Bluebird about to break the world land speed record, Daytona Beach, 1931.*

Right: *Yevonde and cousin Malcolm Campbell at Daytona Beach, 1931.*

Below: *Sir Malcolm Campbell, wife Dolly (who posed for Niobe) and their children Joan and Donald, in 1932.*

21
GODDESSES
& OTHERS

Yevonde's cousin Malcolm Campbell, (not yet Sir Malcolm Campbell) asked her, in February 1931, to go with him to Daytona in Florida where he was to make an attempt to reclaim the world speed record in *The Bluebird*. They knew each other well, at eighteen he had moved in with her family for a while and she spent much time tearing round country roads in an open car driven by her dare-devil cousin. In those days he was always filthy, with hands, clothes and hair covered in thick layers of oil and grease: when he came into a room everyone rushed to put newspaper down on the chairs before he sat down. Her father had financed his first test run – a motor cycle trial from London to Edinburgh – which he won. After serving in the Royal Flying Corps during 1914–18, he established an extremely profitable business insuring newspapers against libel actions. Throughout the 1920s he won over four hundred motor-racing trophies before his attempts on the world land and water speed records. Now he wanted to reclaim the record from Henry Seagrave.

When it sailed for New York, there were few passengers on the *Homeric*. It was the middle of a slump, yet Malcolm's car, built the year before, had cost twenty thousand pounds, ten thousand of which was his own money. *Bluebird* stood on deck in an enormous packing case, weighing three and a half tons and was twenty-five feet long. Both Malcolm and *Bluebird* generated great excitement which Yevonde describes, 'Before we had berthed we were the centre of an army of reporters, photographers and movie cameramen. We were met by the Mayor of New York and driven in decorated cars to the hotel; our suite immediately overflowed with reporters and cameramen'. Then came two days and nights by train to Florida.

On reaching Daytona they had to wait five days for *Bluebird* to arrive by goods train from New York and when it did, large crowds gathered. The nine-mile long beach is composed of sand made from coquina shells, pounded to dust by the Atlantic breakers, which pack the surface hard, firm and smooth. On the day of the trial run, Yevonde witnessed the procession to the beach. 'Preceded by a band of outriders, the *Bluebird* was being towed, with Leo Villa, (chief mechanic) at the wheel. In close attendance were dozens of cameramen and *Movietone News,* and stretching behind, a long line of cars of every make, size and colour; some smart, some shabby, some gleaming, others tied up with string, some driven by chauffeurs, others by cuties and blondes; some driven by men in rags, others by men smoking big cigars, but all out to do homage to Speed'.

The people of Daytona were warned by the sounding of sirens that a speed trial would take place . . . 'when they would stop work and race for the dunes in their cars'. Everyone was nervous except Malcolm, who challenged Yevonde to a game of ping-pong and won. He put in his pocket a box of little mascots and after a conversation with *Movietone News* went off to the start. The band played the Toreador's song from *Carmen* several times before the trial. As he entered the measured mile, the low hum of the engine changed to a tearing shriek as the car flew past in a blue streak. It was announced – "Captain Campbell's speed is 245.736 miles per hour. He has beaten the world record". Before leaving for Washington, where Malcolm had an interview with President Hoover, they picnicked on the Tomoka river watching alligators and turkey buzzards. They then flew to New York, and on landing were introduced to Amelia Earhart, the first woman to fly solo across the Atlantic. Two days later they embarked at

They embarked at midnight on the 'Mauretania'.

midnight on the *Mauretania*.

On board was Charlie Chaplin, and he and Yevonde became good friends. He loved to dance, especially the tango, and always asked Yevonde. Nobody else danced the tango but the two of them, and with everyone watching, Charlie always started giggling, saying "I wish you wouldn't look so serious, it makes me want to laugh". Yevonde would answer, "Do be quiet. If you laugh I shall make a mistake". Then they would dance very solemnly until Charlie started to laugh and they would both dissolve into hopeless giggles. Chaplin had been the supreme comic actor of silent films for fifteen years. He had just made *City Lights* and was anxiously trying to make the transition from silent films to talkies. In the middle of the Atlantic he was sea-sick, and Yevonde went to his stateroom where they talked at length, mostly about politics. She later wrote, "Politically he is, as one would expect, well over to the left, always on the side of the underdog, the weak against the strong, the poor against the rich, the unsuccessful rather than the prosperous, the meek and not the arrogant". All of which, she was in total agreement with.

23
GODDESSES
& OTHERS

Charlie Chaplin dancing the tango in 'City Lights'.

24
GODDESSES
& OTHERS

'Invitation' from The Bystander, Sept. 9th, 1925.

Felia Doubrovska of the Ballets Russes at His Majesty's Theatre, June 1928.

25
GODDESSES
& OTHERS

26
GODDESSES
& OTHERS

This portrait of Mrs Constant Lambert appeared on the cover of 'The Sketch' in March 1933, captioned 'The Exotic Wife of a Composer'.

IV
Fortune Smiles 1932–1935

In 1914 when Yevonde started in business there seemed no hope of taking photographs in colour. Always irritated by the limitations of black and white, she disliked not being able to reproduce what she saw: but in 1930, there was a rumour that colour might soon become a possibility. Deciding she must learn to photograph in colour, Yevonde enquired from commercial travellers what and where this process might be. One or two studios were experimenting with colour, the principal being Dr Spencer's in Willesden, whose colour process was called 'Vivex'. Yevonde contacted the studio and learned that Vivex prints were produced by the subtractive process, which involves making three separate, but identical negatives, which are superimposed for printing. To do this, she had to buy a repeating-back costing thirty pounds to fix on her camera. It held three glass quarter-plates which were pulled, during exposure, behind three coloured glass filters. Exposure was regulated by adjusting taps under each filter, which once fixed, were completely automatic. After exposure the glass negatives were sent to the factory for processing, and she was 'thrilled and delighted to find I received for £2 12s 6d a most glorious fifteen by twelve inch colour print, the print being an exact representation of my lighting and arrangement in the studio.' On her repeating-back camera she had a nine-inch Ross lens she most frequently used at f/5 for three seconds. Her negatives were on the dense side and she always enlarged her quarter plates up to fifteen by twelve inches.

Yevonde felt liberated by the use of colour, exclaiming, "Hurrah, we are in for exciting times. Red hair, uniforms, exquisite complexions and coloured fingernails come into their own". She experimented and found Dr Spencer and his colleagues encouraging and inspiring, always ready with help and advice in interpreting her ideas.

Founded in 1928, Colour Photographs Ltd., at Vivex House, Victoria Road, N.W.10, had begun by 1931 to cater for a few enthusiastic photographers, producing remarkable results for reasonable prices. Dr Spencer's Vivex process resembles the Carbro process. First, the colour separation negatives were printed on a semi-matt bromide paper. A sheet of appropriately coloured pigmented gelatine, sensitised in a solution of potassium ferricyanide, potassium bromide and chromic acid, was rolled into contact with each of the three positives, then dried in contact with Cellophane. Unhardened pigment gelatine was washed away, the resulting yellow, cyan and magenta relief-images transferred, each in register, from the Cellophane to the finished print. By giving the print both factory-controlled conditions and individual consideration, successful and near-permanent results were achieved. At the height of print production, in the mid 1930s, around two hundred photographers were using the Vivex process.

The work at Vivex House divided into two sections – portraiture, pictorial and advertising work, and works of art, medical and scientific record work. In the first section, slight increases or decreases in the printing time of one of the primaries – such as reducing the amount of blue to warm up a flesh tint – produced acceptable results.

27
GODDESSES
& OTHERS

Above left: *Assembling Vivex prints. Local adjustments to register were made by stretching the cellophane manually.*

Above right: *Yevonde with her Vivex Tri-Colour Camera, Model A.*

Below left: *Dr D.A. Spencer, inventor of the Vivex Colour Process by Ron Callender*

Below right: *Sensitizing room at Vivex. Beneath the trays suspended from the ceiling, electric motors rotated pulley-wheels to rock them during sensitization. Rooms were kept at 65° F.*

But in the second, in which every colour must be reproduced exactly in both hue and saturation, extensive retouching of the negatives would be required. Vivex cameras were available too, as well as fully automatic repeating-backs, incorporating three dials controlling each of three exposures from one sixteenth of a second to about five seconds. The Vivex Colour Camera Model A had a Taylor-Hobson Aviar f4.5 lens and exposed three plates at once; weighing twelve pounds it had a double image range finder and was to be used in daylight.

For her colour work Yevonde used the repeating-back and tungsten flood lighting, sometimes putting coloured paper over the lights to get the desired effect, achieving variety with different arrangements of the lamps. She was so excited by her work that she was oblivious to the fact that sitters did not like the results: the general public were as biased as other photographers against the colour photograph. Yevonde felt that most photographers possessed no sense of colour, or what little they had became non-existent through years of seeing tonally: they had become so engrossed in the beauty of light and shade that they thought the colour photograph unnatural. She thought this was rubbish; that in fact colour opened up new vistas, but she had to fight continually for the recognition of colour as a satisfactory medium for portraiture. She also created many still-life fantasies in Vivex colour. Realising that the colour photograph was closer to painting, she had decided to take them in a large size, fifteen inches by twelve, saying, "the colour photograph has to be something precious, not doled out in dozens".

As a pioneer, and well and truly obsessed with colour work, she spent a good deal of money on preparing, and then promoting, the finished work. Coloured materials for backgrounds were necessary, and because primary colours were easy to photograph, but those colours on the edge of the spectrum – blue-green, green-blue, purple, maroon – were more difficult, she often found, after spending a great deal on a lovely piece of fabric, it was no use and had to be scrapped. So she began to use coloured filters over her lights, and covered her camera lens with blue cellophane to achieve a 'cold' effect – the printers protested as the negatives were out of balance. "Don't correct anything – just print" was her reply.

After experimenting with the process for some time, an exhibition to launch the colour work was planned. Yevonde hired the Albany Gallery in Sackville Street in April 1932 for a one-man show. Catalogues were printed and one thousand five hundred invitations dispatched. It attracted a good deal of attention, particularly from the magazines, so for her newly-found commercial colour work she was able to employ a girl full-time to call on the agents and magazines with samples. Colour photographs were becoming popular as magazine covers, calendars and show-cards; it took far longer than portrait work because of the immense amount of detail, but it did pay better. She had done advertising photographs already for *Eno's Fruit Salts* (1925), for *Cerebos Salt* and *Ovaltine* (1928/29) and this was followed by work for *Christie's Lanolin, Daimler, Canadian Food* and *Glyco-Thymaline*. But her relationship with the commercial world was uneasy, later writing that she could not appreciate photographs, however beautiful, when they were used to advertise fur coats or whisky.

Portrait sitters were slow to respond to colour, but eventually they began to appreciate it. One was so delighted she had her drawing room painted to match her colour portrait which Yevonde thought was treating the colour photograph with the respect it deserved. She took actress Joan Maude, with fiery red hair, wearing a cherry coat, against a bright red background, and a corn-coloured blonde in a primrose blouse against a background of different coloured yellows. Then she became interested in using pastel colours, photographing Lady Derwent (who had deep blue eyes) in soft tones of pink and grey, and Lady Beatty in a grey dress against pale grey and green with a red rose in her hand. Many colour originals appeared on the cover of the *Tatler*, *The Sketch* and *The Bystander* in black and white.

The lease on the studio at 100 Victoria Street ran out early in 1933, and Yevonde decided to move to the West End (by which she meant the area enclosed by Bond Street, Park Lane, Oxford Street and Piccadilly). Most of the leading portrait photographers of the day had Bond Street studios – such as Dorothy Wilding, whilst Paul Tanqueray, Bertram Park, Yvonne Gregory and Marcus Adams, were round the corner in Dover Street; although Yevonde looked over a number of premises she didn't like the street enough to move there. Finally she chose Berkeley Square, as she loved the huge, stylish houses, finding a studio at number 28, above Captain Parker's Naval Prints Gallery. Berkeley Square had always fascinated her, and it was much the same as it had been two hundred years before – an eighteenth century pagoda stood in the centre of the square, round which plane trees grew; she found it elegant and charming. "I was to observe other advantages for the Society Photographer" she wrote, "the number of motors, streamlined with long bonnets and silver fittings...and the strolling, slender women with carmine lips and spiky lashes wearing fox furs or summer ermine, made the future appear quite dazzling". She employed a secretary and several assistants.

Her lighting was now with Kodak lamps; three at 3,000 watts, two 500 and one 250, a headlight and some spotlights. In the first few months many familiar sitters came to be photographed at the new studio, pleased that she had moved to a more convenient neighbourhood. They also began to ask her out socially, which she felt was a sure sign of success, and she quickly gained a reputation as a witty dinner guest.

Edgar too had been successful. In 1927, his play *Potiphar's Wife* was produced, with Jean de Cassilis playing the lead, and was soon running to packed houses. It made him eight thousand pounds, which he doubled on the Stock Exchange, before losing all in the slump. He had made a name for himself, however, and wrote other plays, *Tin Gods* in 1928 and a revue the following year *Morning, Noon and Night*. He assembled the first talkie biography of the Prince of Wales in 1933, and wrote Lord Beaverbrook's biography in 1934. He tried to enter politics, standing as a Liberal for East Islington ((inventing telephone canvassing), but was defeated. He continued writing, feeling confident that another success would come; meanwhile Yevonde was the chief breadwinner.

Colour continued to obsess Yevonde, and in December 1932 she gave what was described as a "racy" address to the Royal Photographic Society, entitled "Why Colour?", which outlined the problems of the reproduction of colour particularly in portraiture and speaking from her own experience, which colours should be emphasised or subdued. She talked of the difficulties in achieving successful flesh tones and the use of make-up, the special difficulties in colour portraits of men. (Here she cited the

Yevonde's studio at No. 28 Berkeley Square, occupied the two floors above the Royal Milliner, M. Rita. Her display box is to the left of the entrance.

Berkeley Square in the early 1930's.

Yevonde and Edgar Middleton, 1928.

example of the clergyman with a red nose, which glowed redder and redder under the studio lights, coming to the conclusion that he should be rendered in black and white). "The use of the colour photograph" she declared, "would prove an immense boon to doctors in the photographing of diseases, notably skin diseases at certain stages". She went on to stress that in advertising the colour photograph would eventually be used exclusively, but that the most important factor in the colour workers's equipment was imagination. "Technical efficiency is a commonplace in our modern world, but the man who will use his imagination is a rare creature". The importance of backgrounds was outlined in which she stated, "if we are going to have colour photographs for heaven's sake let's have a riot of colour, none of your wishy-washy hand-tinted effects". In summing up she said, "The colour photograph has arrived, it is here for us to develop and exploit. We have got to aim very high, and it will cost a lot of money and a lot of time. We have not yet touched on its possibilities. We have nowhere to turn for help or guidance – we have no history, no tradition, no Old Masters, but only a future! And that I think is rather exciting".

In the discussion afterwards it was agreed that colour photography had reached its current prominence due to the efforts of one or two "lonely pioneers" like Madame Yevonde who had been prepared to spend money, time, energy and imagination in making both artistic and commercial use of the new medium.

At the end of October, 1935, Lady Alice Christabel Montagu-Douglas-Scott, shortly to become the Duchess of Gloucester, made an appointment to be photographed in her wedding dress four days before the event. Press excitement at the Gloucester wedding was intense for days. News of the sitting leaked out, and there were requests to photograph Yevonde photographing Lady Alice. She refused, but press photographers caught the Scots beauty arriving and leaving the Berkeley Square studio. As the black and white photographs would be used in the newspapers, Yevonde decided on a white background which would reproduce better than a dark one. She bought a new chair for her royal sitter and Constance Spry lent her two carved antique columns on which to arrange flowers. A pearl satin dress with a long train of frilly tulle arrived from Norman Hartnell, who came himself to arrange the head dress. After the black and white shots, Yevonde changed to the colour camera, putting at the bride's feet a sheaf of red roses tied with blue ribbon which she felt were "symbolic of England, love, luck and romance". The pictures were a huge success.

Yevonde had reached a point by the beginning of 1936 when she wanted to specialise in colour work and cut out black and white altogether. The colour photographs had made a name for her in London, but she was impatient for colour to be as accepted in England as it was in America. So in February she took her portfolio to New York to explore the possibilities of America as a market place, visiting the advertising agencies and magazines from whom she already had indications of interest. One such was *Fortune* magazine. At the time, it was a very large format full-colour magazine devoted to business matters, with a circulation of around a hundred and thirty thousand. *Fortune* immediately commissioned her to photograph the liner *Queen Mary* being fitted out at John Brown's yard on the Clyde, and asked her what her fee would be: Yevonde normally charged twenty guineas a picture in her studio, but more for location work. *Fortune* particularly wanted pictures of workmen putting the finishing touches to the Cunard liner, and of the two artist sisters Anna and Doris Zinkeisen at work on decorative panels.

Back home, Yevonde telephoned the Zinkeisens at their London studio (where the decorations were being done to scale) and they gave her disappointing news that they would not be on board again. Then it took a lot of persuading to get permission to photograph the liner. First she was turned down because "photographers delayed work", then when she pointed out that *Fortune* wanted to see men at work, she was told that the men objected to a woman working in the shipyard and she might be subject to rough handling! Yevonde laughed, and tried again through Cunard, who finally agreed to give her access for one day.

One bright Sunday morning in March Yevonde and an assistant were at last in Glasgow on board the most talked-of ship of the day. It took an hour and a half to unload the cameras, slides, tripods, lights and cables. She took with her three cameras – a field camera, single shot colour camera and a repeating-back Vivex model which was used for most of the shots. The only single shot colour camera in England at that time had a long-focus lens, fine for portrait work but impractical for interiors. She was told she must not photograph the port side of the liner. First she took two shots from the quayside with the field camera, changing filters between exposures; then on deck, a shot of the huge funnels. She writes, 'After climbing many steps we emerged on deck, and I shall never forget the vivid beauty of the orange-red funnels against the delicate blue of the spring sky. By the time we had chosen our position and set up the camera and made everything ready, the sun had gone behind an inky cloud and the sky was grey. Heavy clouds were rolling up and the snow-capped mountains in the distance turned purple. In the meadows across the river a farmer had set up a marquee; he was serving hot drinks and sandwiches to those hundreds of motorists who had driven over for a sight of the ship. On the port side, lying quite close, was a half-completed

The Queen Mary, at John Brown's yard, 1936, Vivex by Yevonde

destroyer. There was something rather pathetic, as well as wicked, about this half-formed grey ship, in comparison so small, lying quietly behind the almost completed liner. There was red paint or a red chemical stain smeared down the destroyer's side, giving the impression that blood had already started to flow. Suddenly, out came the sun. I rushed back to the camera and we made an exposure. And then the sun went in for good. It started to rain and we went below'.

Starting in the chapel, where workmen were laying linoleum, the first task was to connect her six six-thousand-watt lights. She connected them up to the fuse box, switched on, and promptly fused all the lights on the ship. An irate superintendent in a bowler hat strode up and fiercely accused Yevonde, "Now see what you've done". But she turned on her considerable charm, and apologising, explained her task. He soon became very interested, and began to help, putting up the altar table for a photograph. The placated superintendent now sent Yevonde an electrician and they moved to the Nursery where carpenters were working. Here was a Wild West shack, sentry box, doll's house, a cinema and aquarium of tropical fish under a painted ceiling of sun, stars and man-in-the-moon. Brown paper was over the small painted furniture.

By eight-thirty it had taken nine hours to get four pictures, but Yevonde wanted more. "I will go to the awful John Brown" she thought. "I will beard the man in his den. I will tell him I need to stay on the ship for two more days". The next morning she boldly asked the door-keeper at the dock gates to see John Brown and was taken to wait in a room hung with photographs of ships. When he appeared she explained, "I know you hate my presence on the Queen Mary. But I'm photographing in colour. It takes so long. I haven't nearly finished". To her surprise he replied kindly that she might stay as long as she liked so long as she didn't photograph the destroyer. Thanking him profusely she skipped out and up the gangway.

It was Monday morning and the ship was crawling with workmen hammering, welding, cutting, sawing, painting, polishing and unpacking. She photographed the observation lounge under the Captain's bridge, the swimming bath, a private dining room, a state-room, some workmen fixing an engraved glass panel in the main tourist lounge, and a little scarlet cocktail-bar filled with cheerful workmen. Then the Zinkeisens arrived after all – alterations were found to be necessary to their decorations – and Yevonde got pictures of them at work. Anna in the dining room surrounded by carpenters and welders said . . . "I'm sure my nose needs powdering but I don't like to do it in front of all these workmen". Doris, embarrassed by the men's interest had erected a sort of tent for protection. Yevonde has meanwhile asked the local Employment Exchange for a boy who knew the ship to help carry lights and cables about; he stammered, and his accent was so Scottish, she could not understand a word he said, and he kept getting lost. But Yevonde felt at home on the ship, distributing toffees (which as no smoking was allowed was very welcome). She had been told she would get nothing done on the Clyde without heavy tipping, yet she did not find one man who would accept a tip; also that the men would be rough, rude and unpleasant, but she found nothing but good manners, good nature and understanding, their attitude being that Yevonde had a job to do like themselves. She had *Fortune*'s deadline to meet, had cut time short for the Vivex prints to be made and so had to leave. Erland Echlin, the

London representative for *Time* and *Fortune* pronounced the pictures "superb" and advised her to send a dozen rather than the four ordered. They thought them "swell" and reproduced the lot in the June 1936 issue.

Whilst at her Victoria Street studio Yevonde had begun a friendship with Lady Rhondda, who, in addition to running her father's Welsh coal-mines, formed the Six Point Group, which continually pressed Members of Parliament for widows' pensions, equal rights of guardianship for both parents and equal opportunities for women in the Civil Service. She organised a Women's Rotary club, called the "Women's Provisional Club" which Yevonde was asked to join.

It was as a result of her connection with the group that she was asked to lecture in Paris in July 1936 at the Second Annual Conference of the Business and Professional Women's Federation. The subject of the Conference, was "Women's work in the world of Business, Science, the Arts and the Professions". It was attended by American lawyers and teachers, the U.S. Minister of Labour, an Indian doctor, a Chinese diplomat, an Italian actuary, Members of Parliament from Norway, Sweden and Czechoslovakia, a German journalist and several Cabinet Ministers. "Women's contribution to the modern world" was the title of the public meeting at which she spoke on photography. Among other speakers were the fashion designer Elsa Schiaparelli (who sent her manager to read her speech), and Miss Gordon Holmes, (a woman stockbroker who ran a bucket shop as women were not allowed on the Stock Exchange). Yevonde's speech dealt first with "Women's stimulating and productive influence in the sphere of photography". She then described Thomas Wedgewood's early experiments with light-sensitive materials, how he soaked paper and leather in a silver and nitrate solution on which he lay a fern which retained an impression. She went on to mention other pioneers, including Julia Margaret Cameron, before talking about colour photography. Her speech ended by her pointing out that photography was both an art and a science, a business and a profession. It was well received.

That evening there was a public meeting on the subject of "Government and Employment". The speeches were to be broadcast to America, and the hall was packed, flashlight photographs were being taken and *Movietone News* shone powerful lights on both speakers and audience creating an atmosphere of anticipation. But when Madame Cecile Brunshwigg, French cabinet minister and Under-secretary for Education, rose to make her speech, a group of French women stood on chairs and broke into shouts of "Les femmes de France veulent voter". The British delegates immediately understood what was happening having adopted the same policy of refusing any Cabinet minister the right of uninterrupted public speech during their suffrage movement. In France in 1936 women could sit in Parliament though they could not vote! "Quite right, they are quite right", Miss Gordon Holmes shouted in her stentorian voice through the mayhem.

On the last evening was a banquet, and a couple of hours before Yevonde was told she must give another speech after it. The President of the Federation, told her that her lecture was so enjoyable that they wanted her to speak after dinner on the subject of "If I were a Dictator". Yevonde had not the courage to refuse and was flattered at the honour, though there were to be two hundred and fifty women at dinner (and two men) and it was to be reported in the press. Although she had lectured several times, she felt a great intellectual gulf between herself and the other women with trained minds and experience in public life. So she decided not to take it seriously, and, wearing a navy blue taffeta dress with white spots, delivered a speech on the subject of Mickey Mouse as dictator who did absurd and amusing things like introducing compulsory travel and compulsory international marriage. Said in fun and taken in fun, she found that the press had taken it seriously, one paper writing a jeering leader and she eventually found herself in *The Daily Express*'s Beachcomber column. However, it was a boost to Yevonde's career, she found the ideas stimulating and she also found it interesting to compare the different national groups. The British delegates were the jolliest, the most carefree and confident: the Americans were serious and sincere: the French melancholic and reserved. She recaptured her enthusiasm of the suffragette days, 'when votes for women seemed also to mean the reform of the world – that is, disease and poverty would be abolished, and the marriage problem settled for all time'.

In April 1937, Yevonde was commissioned to photograph in colour the Duke and Duchess of Kent with their young son, Edward, and newly-born daughter Princess Alexandra. At the Kent's house in Belgrave Square the nurse brought Princess Alex into the drawing room where Yevonde had arranged some blue and green star-covered satin: it was to be the Princess's first photograph for which she behaved perfectly; Prince Edward's liveliness made his portrait difficult. The *Sketch* published Yevonde's picture of the family group in their April 28th issue.

Colour photography was in demand for George VI's coronation on May 12th, 1937, and Yevonde was commissioned to do a number of peers and peeresses in their robes. Beforehand, she had confessed to Norman Hartnell her worries over the difficulties involved, for the crimson velvet would require long exposures, which would burn out the white of the ermine. Hartnell sent a lovely mannequin wearing a kirtle and train over a long dress round to Berkeley Square for her to experiment with lighting and backgrounds. She found dark backgrounds required too long an exposure but a light background and foreground worked best, reflecting light onto the velvet. Lord Louis Mountbatten, (whom Yevonde describes as 'the number one pin-up boy of the time') and Lady Edwina came to the studio to be photographed but they had silk robes. Yevonde went to St James' Palace to photograph the Gloucesters, then the Northumberlands as a large family group. She noticed that Lady Swathling had the pockets of her robes lined with oiled silk to act as containers for chocolate and raisins.

Mrs Edward Mayer as Medusa, 1935.

Left: *Mrs Michael Balcon as Minerva, 1935.*

Right: *Lady Bridget Poulett as Arethusa, 1935.*

Right: *Mrs Richard Hart-Davis as Ariel, 1935.*

Left: *Mrs Richard Hart-Davis as Andromeda, 1935.*

Actress Mary Ellis in Victor Stiebel, July 1933.

37
GODDESSES
& OTHERS

Yevonde's portrait of the Duchess of Gloucester in her Hartnell wedding-dress, 1935

Isobel McLean, August 1934.

40
GODDESSES
& OTHERS

Anna Zinkeison painting a mural on the Queen Mary, 1936.

Lady Anne Rhys as Flora, 1933. Vivex Colour original.

Lady in a fur stole, 1933, Vivex Colour original.

Lady Weymouth, 1935. Vivex Colour original.

Lady with Violets, 1934, Vivex Colour original.

41
GODDESSES
& OTHERS

42
GODDESSES
& OTHERS

THE ART OF THE CAMERA
AT ITS BEST

THE HON. MRS. JAMES BECK AND (ON RIGHT AND BELOW) HER DAUGHTER, MISS DIANA BETHELL

Miss Diana Bethell is very like her beautiful mother, the Hon. Mrs. James Beck, who is Lord Glenconner's only sister, and Captain Adrian Bethell's former wife. Captain Bethell's connection with the Holderness country as an M.F.H. dates back to 1928, when he was first joint-Master with Major Newland Hillas. They are still the Masters on the Holderness side. The Holderness is a country of wide ditches, very deep, and the locals have a way of saying that you are not really "in" if even your nose is above water

MISS DIANA BETHELL

Hon. Mrs James Beck as Daphne, 1935

V
Goddesses and Others: 1935–1946

In May 1936, Yevonde gave rather a gloomy lecture to the Royal Photographic Society which was published in the *British Journal of Photography* entitled 'The Future of Portraiture – If Any'. The title was not of her own choosing. She attributed the steady falling off in the demand for portrait photographs to several new situations. Firstly the competition from store photographs (Photomaton and Polyfoto); the work of the energetic amateur, with new, smaller cameras and cheaper, improved films; smaller families, living in smaller houses, who saw each other more frequently; lastly she felt, the novelty of being photographed had worn off. To combat their effects, Yevonde suggested that professional studio portraits should be more original than ever by turning to the history of art for ideas. The personal touch was essential, to be as different in atmosphere from the store photograph as possible. She cited her own back-to-back idea of presenting photographs as a 'stunt' that caught on. To combat amateur competition, the war must be carried into the enemy camp by also using a smaller camera. Falling-off in the size of orders must be countered by higher prices, but the work must be outstandingly good. Of colour portraits, she drew a parallel with films, where black and white was being ousted. "Colour portraiture demands constructive purpose and sustained effort" she declared, and concluded with a plea for photographers to put life and colour into their work.

By way of a house-warming for the Berkeley Square studio, Yevonde decided to hold an exhibition of new colour work. She believed exhibitions were helpful to the exhibitor because the effort required stimulates the imagination, and the need to produce important work to a deadline generates a concentration which gives startlingly good results. If the photographer feels he has stretched himself to produce something better than ever, then the object of the show is achieved.

Having turned to paintings for inspiration in the past, Yevonde had been mulling over for some time the eighteenth century painters' idea of persuading beauties of the day to represent Greek goddesses and had portrayed Lady Anne Rhys as *Flora* in 1933. Yevonde herself had always had leanings towards a world of fantasy and make-believe, and dressing up was always a part of her life. In fact she had been delivered into the world by a doctor dressed as one of Louis XVI's courtiers, on his way to a fancy dress ball. When taking self-portraits, she always dressed as someone else, for her the idea of being an imposter was as exciting in visual imagery as it is in literature. There had been an 'Olympian Ball' at Claridges on March 5th, 1935, organised by Olga Lynn in aid of the Greater London Fund for the Blind. Celebrities and society people appeared as deities and mythological personages in costumes designed by Oliver Messel, Cecil Beaton, Eleanor Abbey and Derek Hill which were featured in *The Tatler* and *The Bystander*. Yevonde was never happy with the outfits her sitters came to the studio to be photographed in, so to shoot beautiful sitters in fantasy costumes was her ideal subject.

She called her show 'An Intimate Exhibition – Goddesses and Others'. It ran from

July 3rd to the 20th, 1935, in the afternoons at the Berkeley Square studio; there were spreads in *The Bystander* and *The Sketch*. Yevonde had chosen as Medusa the beautiful Mrs Edward Mayer, wife of the film director; she had intensely deep blue and rather strange eyes. As Medusa was a cold voluptuary and a sadist, Yevonde wanted to achieve very cool tones, which she created by first painting her model's lips purple and her face chalk-white, then placing a green filter over one of the lights. For the snakes around Medusa's head and neck, Yevonde sent out Mrs Ken Wood, her props. assistant, for bright green rubber snakes, but none of London's toy shops had them. Among Yevonde's many friends were artists to whom she often turned for accessories for her photographs. This time they made her some little adders of black tape bound around wire, with gold beads for eyes and forked tongues of gold wire, but they were too small and too few for Medusa's head-dress. Then, whilst walking along the Strand, Yevonde saw a man selling bright green rubber snakes in the street; they had a hole in the tail for inflation and were sixpence each. She bought twelve, but when inflated, they looked more like small green car tyres than writhing snakes. So they were painted a dull greenish black, making them more evil than ever, and the insertion of a wire through a cord made them writhe at will. Sequins made their eyes, and with the little black adders she completed the head-dress and posed Medusa against a vaguely sinister and unevenly-lit background to achieve the desired effect.

For the goddess Niobe, a model with beautiful eyes was required. Yevonde asked Lady Dolly Campbell. Niobe was the proud mother of six sons and six daughters of whom she boasted and praised so much that, in jealousy, they were all killed. The god Jupiter turned her to stone and she wept incessantly for her children. Yevonde wanted to take a close-up of a face expressive of misery and suffering, with no symbolic accessories or background. She thought that tears in Hollywood films were made of glycerine, but found the glycerine rolled too quickly down Dolly's cheeks, so she mixed vaseline in with it, but it became lumpy and not transparent. So more glycerine was used which got in Dolly's eyes and, mixing with her mascara, caused agonizing pain. When she was able to look up again, her bloodshot eyes and genuine expression of utter misery was exactly right, and Yevonde rushed to focus her lens to capture a shot like a film-still, reminiscent of Man Ray's 'Tears'.

Daphne, the nymph surprised by Apollo while bathing, who on praying for deliverance was turned into a laurel bush, was the Hon. Mrs Beck. Yevonde got the effect of face-into-laurel-leaves by double-printing the leaves over the face. Lady Milbanke posed as Penthesilea, the Amazon Queen. Unlike Inigo Jones' Penthesilea, Yevonde insisted on a leopard-skin and the idea of a leopard-skin choker to support Achilles' arrow piercing her throat. She is about to fall back dead, with closed eyes.

Arethusa, who prayed for deliverance from the disillusionment of love, was changed into a fountain that went underground and became the spirit that broods near ponds and streams, was Lady Bridget Poulett. There are two versions of Arethusa: one full length, in a green dress and holding bulrushes, the hair entwined with long green fake bulrush-leaves flowing out behind, as if in water; the other a head looking down at a border of glass fishes, the leaves flowing upwards. For this shot Yevonde put green cellophane over the camera lens, which took out all the warm tones and gave a watery-greenish look to the skin. It upset the balance of the three negatives and the printers protested, but it was exactly the effect she wanted.

Moon goddess Hecate, who watches over travellers and childbirth, is represented in classical art with three heads for the full, waxing and waning moon. A soft grey net was thrown over the Duchess of Wellington's head and Yevonde set her full-face against a grey background with a single star. Three separate prints were mounted together for the three-headed effect.

For Psyche, Yevonde chose her friend Mrs Dorothy Gisborne, who had dark eyes with fair hair and an exquisite mouth which she felt expressed both the pleasure and the pain that Psyche had to endure when Aphrodite, jealous of her beauty, ordered her son Eros (the god of love) to make her fall in love with the worst of men, but he fell in love with her himself. Mrs Anthony Eden posed as the muse of History in a classical wig, and Gertrude Lawrence as the muse of Lyric Poetry in little more than a veil, some flowers and a guitar.

The picture that took most effort to assemble was Europa (daughter of the King of Tyre, carried off by Jupiter in the form of a bull, who so fascinated her by his beauty and tameness, she mounted his back and rode away). Mrs Donald Ross was chosen for Europa, but it was necessary to find a stuffed bull. They tried first the Natural History Museum, who were scandalised that they should want to take a bull away from a museum and put it in a photographer's studio. Then they telephoned Bovril, who were no help as their bull had been destroyed by moths. Then they tried Rowland Ward, who pointed out that the bull, as a domestic animal was never stuffed. Colonial and travel bureaux offered moose, elk and antelope, but finally, film people put them on to the Camden Town emporium of stuffed animals, who hired them out by the day or week. Here was a stuffed bull to pose with Europa. Euterpe, Circe, Ceres, Ariadne, Persephone, Dido, Hebe, Helen of Troy and Venus were added to the collection.

Yevonde had not only looked to classical art for her ideas, but to contemporary art also – surrealism was in the air. The following summer more than twenty thousand people queued to visit the International Surrealist Exhibition at the New Burlington Galleries (where Salvador Dali appeared in a diving suit covered in plasticine hands, with a car radiator cap on his head, and carrying a billiard cue accompanied by two Irish wolfhounds). Through her admiration of the photographic work of Man Ray, Yevonde took an interest in the movement which had been originated towards the end of the Great War by European poets and artists. In 1924 André Breton had published a surrealist manifesto and the movement continued through what Patrick Waldberg has called "a time of euphoria and extravagance", the late 1920s and early 1930s. Between 1930 and 1936 Man Ray had produced a series of exquisite black and white portrait photographs of Meret Oppenheim, Lee Miller and Dora Maar and published his 'Photographs 1920 – 1934' which Yevonde found exciting. The unconscious, dreams, chance and automatism outline the mode of surrealism and it was the dream-like imagery of the slightly irrational that Yevonde brought to her goddess images. She continued to produce them over the next three years, and other colour studies including a nude at a sewing machine.

Planning a further series of colour portraits, based on the signs of the Zodiac, she

46
GODDESSES
& OTHERS

Advertisement for Canadian Food, 1933, Vivex Colour original.

47
GODDESSES
& OTHERS

'Crisis, 1939', Vivex Colour original.

left a note asking for a virgin, a scorpion and a stuffed wasp on Mrs Ken Wood's desk, who, pink, with indignation, rebelled, expostulating "Really!" for the rest of the day. So Yevonde had to find them herself; first a prim porcelain antique virgin figure and an artificial wasp in Bond Street; in the window of a shop opposite the British Museum she 'saw a man-eating spider', so, going in, asked for a stuffed scorpion. There were drawers full.

But her plans and efforts were all in vain, for circumstances were conspiring to prevent her from pursuing her beloved colour work. First, towards the end of 1938, Edgar fell ill. He grew worse and liver cancer was diagnosed; he went steadily downhill and died on the 10th April 1939. He was forty-four, a disappointed man. His last play, *England Expects* was enthusiastically received in Coventry but when transferred to Hampstead was a flop. The autobiography which he published in 1935 bore the unencouraging title *I Might Have Been a Success*. A last book, *Men Who are Shaping the Future* was published posthumously. After Yevonde had scattered Edgar's ashes under the magnolia tree below their window in the Temple gardens, she packed up her things in her home of twenty years. Despite Edgar's shortcomings, she missed him terribly, and couldn't bear to stay.

That summer the threat of war hung over Europe, and in September war was declared. Yevonde did one last colour picture "Crisis – 1939", a still-life of a Roman portrait head wearing a gas mask beside some red geraniums. She wrote, "the year 1939 has been a tragic one for me personally as well as for the world". The outbreak of war caused the Vivex factory to close down, most of its staff went into the armed forces, and the company was wound up.

For two months there were no sitters at the studio. After moving her home and cats to a garden flat in Frobisher House in the newly-built Dolphin Square, Yevonde wondered if she could carry on at the Berkeley Square studio through another war. She felt very frightened, as suddenly she was very much alone; but finally determined that she would remain and that Hitler and his bombs would not chase her away. Her autobiography *In Camera* had just been published by John Gifford and there would be soldiers to photograph, she reasoned. Gradually, a thin trickle of sitters, nearly all men, came for their pictures – colonels, cadets, subalterns, admirals, war office officials and men from the ranks.

But her new home was heavily bombed. No one knew quite why Dolphin Square received so many bombs: some speculated that it was due to its proximity to the river, others that it was so close to Battersea Power Station and the Gas Works; another theory was that its vast size made the German pilots think it was a government building or barracks. Ironically the complex had been inspired by the 'castle' idea – a living environment with all amenities to be resistant to siege. The first bomb fell into the shelter killing over thirty people, then the garage was hit destroying five hundred cars. One morning, as she was about to go to the studio, she heard a noise of gun-fire coming nearer. From the window she saw her black cat streaking towards her, ears back with an expression of terror. It dived through the window and together they fled to the hall, as the bomb came down and exploded in the lift shaft.

One night there was a very bad raid, making it too noisy to sleep and Yevonde went

Left: *Mrs Donald Ross as Europa, 1935.*

Right: *Elizabeth Cowell. Portrait on her appointment as one of the two first announcers for BBC television, May 1936.*

Left: *Actress Joan Maude in red, 1931.*

Right: *Lady Diana Abdy, who had a reputation for choosing chic and amusing hats (here a circle of felt on a skein of wool) April, 1936.*

Lady Dolly Campbell as Niobe, 1935.

down to a shelter for the first time. It was full of people fully dressed and made-up, some in fur coats, lying on rather smart mattresses and lilos. Growing bored of leaning against the wall, she went up into the garden. The sky was purple and crimson from the fires and full of sparks, pigeons were flying round and round above them. As she watched, she heard a sound as if "forty thousand pigs were screaming in anguish", and running to the river bank, saw that the Gas Works had received a direct hit. They were blazing fiercely and the strange screaming came from the safety valves which prevented explosion.

A few days later a bomb struck the top of Frobisher House at night. After the impact, the noise of things falling seemed to go on for hours, and at the bottom Yevonde thought she would be buried. Then there was total silence, total darkness and the noise of water rushing in. Her door was jammed but the wardens came and let her out, as the air was suffocating with dust and fumes. Yevonde found her torch and helped a couple in pyjamas who were soaked to the skin, giving them towels, dry clothes and whisky, and settling them down in her own bed. She lit candles and got out a methylated spirit stove on which to make tea for her now homeless neighbours. Her own flat was not much damaged but she lost several items, including the day-book of studio sitters for the previous decade. After the raid, as the only inhabitable flat, it was frightening to live in total darkness with all the doors and windows blown out. Fortuitously, Yevonde received a letter from her old housekeeper in Farnham who knew of a cottage for sale.

Yevonde and nephew Peter Keighley-Peach, in The Bomb, 1949 at her Bear Lane studio, Farnham.

Exhausted from lack of sleep, the idea of peaceful nights was irresistible, so she went to inspect the cottage which was outside the town, on the edge of a little wood. She bought it, moved in, and the peace and quiet revived her spirits. She became a commuter, travelling up to the studio every day and, for weekends, she opened another studio in an oast-house in Bear Lane, Farnham.

Many families, who had also moved out of London to escape the bombing, came to be photographed. One night a week she had to stay at the Berkeley Square studio and do fire-watching duty which was compulsory. It was very lonely in the huge old house, where she slept on the sofa, but if anything had happened she was on the spot to inform the authorities. In the mornings she went round to have breakfast at Claridges, the Ritz or Lyons Corner House which had, she declared, the best breakfast.

There was a surprising amount of portrait work during the war years – men and women in uniform or their best outfits, sending pictures to their loved ones in faraway places. But when the war ended and soldiers came home, there was still rationing, and practically no-one wanted to be photographed. So in 1946 Yevonde decided to broaden the scope of the studio by finding a partner who did other types of photography. She had good contacts with industrialists amongst her sitters, and as she herself had successfully undertaken the Queen Mary project, she decided that the business could diversify in this direction. Through Ilford, she found a young photographer, Maurice Broomfield, who was also a painter and designer. Together they set up as Yevonde and Broomfield, operating from Berkeley Square and the Bear Lane studios.

Broomfield admired Yevonde and her photography enormously; her Vivex work had made her a celebrity in the photographic world. She, in turn, liked him, his work and his tireless enthusiasm, and the two created a successful partnership. He felt it was hopeless to go round commercial outlets with still photographs trying to procure work. The film strip, which was still in its infancy, was, he suggested, a lucrative idea whereby clients could be offered something of value, through which it was possible to educate. Through Yevonde's contacts with the captains of industry orders were placed, and the studio's main source of revenue in the lean post-war years came to be from the making of film-strips for educational purposes. In the Berkeley Square studio Broomfield built a rostrum camera by converting a cine camera, and an animated bench for tracking. Their subjects were industrial topics, the history of art and design, graphic design, and aspects of biology, chemistry, agriculture and medicine. But more than the work, he remembers delightful weekends he and his wife spent at the Farnham cottage with 'Vondie' and her friend Willie Rhondas, a Belgian fabric designer and muralist. Yevonde (a hopeless cook) would serve Harrods' game pies surrounded by her numerous Persian cats.

Eventually the portrait work and the commercial work got in the way of each other, and the darkroom was far too small, so Maurice Broomfield left the partnership of six years for larger premises in Highgate.

Broomfield assembling material for film-strips at the Berkeley Square studio, 1949.

51
GODDESSES
& OTHERS

Duke and Duchess of Kent, Princess Alexandra and Prince Edward, April, 1937.

52
GODDESSES
& OTHERS

Paul Robeson. c.1930.

Rebecca West posed often for Yevonde and was a close friend, 1929.

John Gielgud as Richard of Bordeaux.

Vivien Leigh. Vivex Colour original. c.1935.

VI
Doves and Predators 1946–1975

When the war ended, Yevonde decided to move back into London as she had grown tired of commuting and wanted to be nearer to Berkeley Square. After finding a big house on Campden Hill, Kensington, she sold the Farnham cottage and studio. At 33, Bedford Gardens, she let the ground floor to Maurice Broomfield and his wife and baby son; Yevonde and her cats occupied the upper floors where she set up a fully-equipped darkroom. She loved the street with its oak, ash and beech trees, flowering shrubs, and climbers growing over the balconies of studios where artists and writers lived and worked.

Something of the atmosphere of Bedford Gardens is conveyed in her own account, "The neighbours are interesting and unobtrusive, virtues which make it easy to love them. But for a while, that explosive firework and film star, Richard Harris, lived in this road. He celebrated his arrival with a noisy 'moving in' party, which finished with a Shakespearean recitation from the top of a motor car at four am, puntuated by cheers from happy guests. Some of the residents were highly scandalised; many had children who were awakened. The next day I was asked by my friends to join with them to have Richard Harris summoned before the Beak as a disturber of the peace. I refused. I said that every dog ought to be allowed one bite, but if the disturbance went on for a week I would co-operate. Nothing was done but many neighbours telephoned Richard Harris and complained. He retaliated. He paid a man to walk up and down ringing a bell and carrying a sandwich board. On this was written 'Love your neighbour Richard Harris'".

Other new neighbours, such as Ronald Searle and Thor Heyerdahl came to be sitters at the studio, and young actresses such as Joan Collins and Kay Kendall, but Yevonde needed to bring in more work to keep the business running. The day of the studio portrait was almost over, and though she was always endeavouring to find ways to promote her business, it was clear that she would have to take her camera out to people rather than have sitters come to her. So, additionally, Ronald Searle was photographed at work in his studio and Thor Heyerdahl writing *American Indians in the Pacific* in his study at 55, Bedford Gardens.

Early in 1951, through her friendship with Lady Georgina Coleridge, then editor of *Homes and Gardens* magazine, she procured commissions to do portraits of people in their own homes, together with a written description of the house, which made three-page features. Accompanied by two of her three assistants, Margaret Biggart, Susan Hoyle and Paula Gisborne, she captured the interiors of houses and their owners from Chelsea to Highgate. But she was only able to use colour in her written captions, not in her camera. Margaret remembers that these occasions were dreaded by the assistants, as they had to both carry an enormous and heavy bag containing the MPP camera, together with the Rolleiflex, tripods, lights, stands, films and junction boxes, and also change plugs when they got there, moving the lot from room to room. One such was at Lionel Bart's house where Willie Rhondas had done a mural of a pastoral scene.

For the coronation of Elizabeth II Yevonde was commissioned to do portraits and family groups in colour. Some, such as the Northumberland family, she had done for the 1937 coronation in Vivex, but in 1953 she used colour negative film in her Rolleiflex.

But the real opportunities to work in colour, which Norman Parkinson found, were across the Atlantic, as Yevonde well knew. Times were changing: at a session to photograph the Archbishop of Canterbury Dr Fisher, in his coronation robes at Lambeth Palace, she was swamped by dozens of press photographers copying her every shot, then bumped into by Cecil Beaton arriving to take a picture for *Vogue* magazine. The lease on Berkeley Square was to expire in 1955 and Yevonde would be sixty-two but couldn't face the idea of retiring. As the area was much changed and the rent would go up alarmingly, she decided to move.

Her agent, Ruby Bernstein, found her a studio at 16a Trevor Street in Knightsbridge, which she immediately loved. It had been a coach house for the huge mansion facing the barracks: large, lofty and light, quiet and separated from the road by a small courtyard, it was a bare shell of a place. But she obtained a lease and set about creating a new studio by covering the floor, installing heating, erecting a dark cupboard for loading and unloading slides and a firm work bench for the dry mounting machine. A platform was built at the top of a flight of stairs for her retoucher, Miss Elliott, who sat with her head under a dark cloth, working on negatives.

Yevonde found the studio ideal for giving exhibitions and also for lunching at Harrods with her friends – Lady Joan Shawcross (her cousin), Sylvia Marshall, with whom she'd worked on the land, Mary Newberry, school friend and daughter of the head of Glasgow School of Art. For portraits the studio had rather too much top-light, but when properly controlled with blinds, and with additional lamps to give side lighting she found this very helpful. Her first project was to photograph every child in Bedford Gardens outside their own house. She then held an exhibition to raise funds for the Save the Children Fund, showing photographs of children living all over the world in not such comfortable circumstances.

After mastering the new lighting set-up at the studio she itched to experiment with what she now considered to be the "sometimes stifling art of portraiture". So when some curious patterns like a mackerel sky formation appeared on the negatives, the effect of which she liked, she approached Kodak to try to establish a scientific basis for the effect. But they were unable to help, and so she decided to learn to make solarized portraits, the technique which Man Ray had used for some superb portraits in the 1930s. Using solarization she photographed the painter Annigoni, the writer Rebecca West, the mime artist Marcel Marceau (whom she declared uninteresting and histrionic), actress Judi Dench, debs, socialites and titled ladies. She photographed them against a black background lit by a strong light, giving a long exposure. During development, which was done by Myrtle Oxland, the film was flashed with white light and the results were quite unpredictable, due to Yevonde's often erratic exposures.

Before the solarization experiments, Yevonde had developed a theory that women fall roughly into two groups, Doves and Predators, (a third species, Birds of Paradise, including Cleopatra, Gaby Deslys and Catherine of Russia had died with emancipation). She decided to divide her sitters into these groups, and acquired a dazzling white dove

55
GODDESSES
& OTHERS

Above left: *Yevonde in her Trevor Street Studio, 1961.*

Above right: *The Knightsbridge Studio at Trevor Street in 1968.*

Left: *Maurice Broomfield's portrait of Yevonde outside her Campden Hill house at 33, Bedford Gardens in 1955.*

and a stuffed hawk to use in the photographs. Solarized portraits presented the sitter in a whole new light, recording cloth and skin texture in a decorative way. She enjoyed the experimenting and the subsequent exhibition and party held at Trevor Street in June 1961. Sitters preferred her ordinary photographs but it was good publicity as it was reported widely, including a feature in *The Tatler* and a column by Auberon Waugh in *The Daily Telegraph*.

It was chiefly a diversion for herself, for she could not help but be bored by the "straight" portraiture she had produced for so long and was still doing – engaged couples, their names culled from *The Times* and *The Telegraph* columns (which Tessa Codrington remembers doing), looked up in Debrett's, and black and white prints sold for ten guineas to *Country Life, Tatler,* or *Londoners' Diary*.

The colour magazines of the early sixties and their extensive use of colour documentary photographs made Yevonde wish she had been born later. "If I were to start a career in photography today" she wrote, "I think I would join the hand camera brigade and wander over the earth and see strange places and unusual faces, or be a nature photographer and photograph birds and animals; I might even go under the sea and photograph fish, corals, anemones and plant life. In my young day, there were not so many aids to this exciting kind of photography, besides it was at that time for me exciting enough to embark on *any* career. The enormous lenses, heavy cameras, fifteen by twelve inch glass plates, monstrous arc lamps and immobile studios seemed to me quite wonderful and I asked for nothing else".

At the age of seventy-two, Yevonde was invited to stay in Ethiopia and she thought it a good opportunity to do a portrait of her hero, Haile Selassie, having for years admired his fine face. She wrote off for permission and, deciding to do the thing in style, took her assistant of some years, Ann Forshaw. She took her M.P.P. camera, several lenses, a Rolleiflex and some Kodalights. Yevonde also procured an assignment to photograph the British Embassy in Addis Ababa for *Homes and Gardens*. On arrival in Addis she went with letters of introduction to arrange an appointment at the Menelik Palace, from where all business was conducted; the Emperor lived at the Jubilee Palace (built to resemble Buckingham Palace). She was told that "H.I.M." was tired and resting in the country, and when he did return, there was a state visit by the German President. Whilst waiting, she explored and photographed the city – huge modern buildings built beside tiny round huts straggling and unplanned on mountain tops, eight thousand feet above sea level, with roads leading to forests, deserts, huge rivers and strange ruins. There were wild animals and exotic birds, and tame lions around the Imperial Palace. She photographed the Pankhurst Museum (where Sylvia's son Richard was the director) and the British Embassy, with its own Sudanese guard, its sloping terraced gardens under eucalyptus, acacia, juniper, pine and fir trees. Here the Ambassador, Sir John Russell, gave a lunch for Yevonde on a terrace under orange trees, after which she photographed the polo ponies. The next day she was given an appointment to photograph the Emperor, and they were met at the Menelik Palace in an atmosphere of awe and agitation, and told in hushed whispers that His Majesty would be ready in five minutes. Whilst the lights were being arranged, Yevonde was led through a series of enormous rooms into the presence of the Negus, the Lion of Judah, seated on a throne,

In the Pankhurst Museum, Addis Ababa.   *Yevonde and lions in Addis Ababa, 1964.*

57
GODDESSES
& OTHERS

where she was presented. Claimed to be the direct descendant of the union between Solomon and the Queen of Sheba, he was charming, but his air of kingship alarmed her, and she found it difficult not to be flustered in his presence. In uniform, he posed in front of the throne, standing and holding a book. But he was very stiff and formal and Yevonde knew that the pictures would be very wooden. So she told him she was very disappointed not to see the little dog that she had heard always shared the throne during cabinet meetings. "It is here" he said, moving aside to reveal a little Chibua curled up at the back of the throne. Yevonde made a noise like a cat which woke "Lulu" up, barking. Everyone laughed and Yevonde, switching to colour, made some more exposures, and then they had to stop. One the way out the lions allowed her to scratch their ears.

Back at the studio, she decided to hold another exhibition, this time of distinguished women, to coincide with the 50th Anniversary of Women's Suffrage. Fifty-three portraits in colour and black and white were assembled, some done especially for the show. There was an altercation at cross-purposes when Iris Murdoch arrived in the rain wearing an old mac and a headscarf, was mistaken by Yevonde for the new cleaning lady and was bartered down in price and set about her tasks. There were her regular sitters, such as Rebecca West, Lady Mountbatten, Princess Marina of Kent, Helen, Duchess of Northumberland; then artists and writers Elizabeth Jane Howard, Barbara Hepworth, Laura Knight, Molly Bishop, the Zinkeison sisters; actresses Gertrude Lawrence, Athene Seyler, Edith Evans, Dorothy Tutin, Susan Hampshire, Olivia Hussey, and other achievers such as Joy Adamson, Christine Truman, Jane Bown, Barbara Castle, Judge Elizabeth Lane and Nancy, Lady Astor. Over the mantelpiece was hung "Eve", a huge (five feet by four) black and white print specially taken for the show. Against a background of leaves and clutching a large serpent (procured from the same Camden Town emporium as the bull) a very pretty model was nude to the waist.

Cecil Beaton came to Trevor Street to see the show, wearing a wide-brimmed hat and made everyone giggle with his remarks. Madame persuaded him to pose for a portrait, which he returned, with "Too much like last year's turkey" written on the back. Yet Yevonde thought him melancholic, and felt that his superb career should have made him happier, and in his old age he should feel joyful to have produced such beautiful work.

The "Distinguished Women" show was meant to have a huge splash in the *The Times* on the day of its opening; women's page editor Sue Puddefoot had done a long interview with Madame and procured many pictures, but a sudden newspaper strike that day left it a much smaller spread on the following day. However, *The Tatler* did a feature and it was widely reported. In March 1969 Yevonde wrote to Sir Roy, then Dr Strong at the National Portrait Gallery, "I am now considering drawing in my horns a bit and going into semi-retirement for the twentieth time. I have a number of negatives that need to be stored or something. I am willing to make them over to you". The lease was to expire on the Trevor Street studio and the ten thousand negatives and hundreds of prints needed a home. The N.P.G. took nearly two hundred prints for their collection, and the Royal Photographic Society acquired others. Mark Gerson now printed her photographs.

At this time Yevonde, who always had immense zest for life, was well-read, very enthusiastic and quite fascinating to be with, began to show signs of vagueness on odd days. Arriving late at the studio (which was very out of character) her assistants suspected that she had had a series of mild strokes. Her assistant Susan Hoyle remembers that her hats would always betray her mood. She always wore a hat; those with long pheasant feathers sticking up would indicate a good mood, when she would be enormous fun and very endearing. A floppy wool beret might indicate a difficult day when she could be awkward, unreasonable and rude, even to the sitters. If she found sitters interesting she would take an hour, using different lighting arrangements, talking animatedly throughout and charming everyone. Those sitters who dared to be uninteresting were dismissed in half an hour. Paula Gisborne remembers an occasion when a society lady turned up to be photographed with six new expensive dresses, asking Yevonde what she thought of them. "They're all perfectly dreadful" she replied, and sent the poor creature back home with an assistant to choose something else. The problem was that not just her health, but her business life – which meant everything to her – were dwindling. The business was her life, the whole aura of the studio a driving force for living.

In 1973 she was eighty, and the Royal Photographic Society of which she had been a member for fifty-eight years, presented a huge show of her work at their gallery in South Audley Street, from mid May to the end of June. Entitled "Sixty years a Portrait Photographer", nearly a hundred prints were mounted. Whilst the show was being organised by Ronald Callender and her last two assistants, Kathy Biggar and Ann Forshaw, her health deteriorated; she had breast cancer and was in and out of hospital. But she decided one last portrait was necessary to inject some topicality into the show. She phoned Sir Alec Douglas-Home, (Foreign Secretary at the time) and explained that she "required a notable personage to sit for her current collection". He agreed to come to Bedford Gardens for fifteen minutes: he arrived punctually accompanied by three body-guards and the huge and ancient camera was wheeled out again. The R.P.S. opening was a gala occasion, the pictures looked superb and Yevonde was buoyant, giving a speech acknowledging that she had given the planners of her birthday present a hard time. *The Observer* colour magazine produced a lively five-page colour feature.

Soon after this, she was invited to appear on *The Frost Programme*. Cautious of David Frost, she asked Ron Callender to go with her. Before the programme in the hospitality suite Ron Callender overheard Yevonde tell Frost that she did not want any of his "smart tricks" and the two professionals agreed a compact. She need not have worried as he coaxed a witty performance out of her.

Encouraged by Kathy Biggar, Yevonde was preparing a lecture to give at the 75th anniversary of the then Institute of Incorporated Photographers (which she had joined in 1919) when she had to go back into St Stephen's Hospital, Fulham. She died there of cancer on 22nd December 1975. Her niece Chloe was with her, and she organised a wake at the Bedford Gardens house, where Yevonde's photographs were displayed. Early in the new year, fifty sad friends gathered for a celebration of her life. Dr Neville Goodman gave a humorous eulogy followed by everyone relating their fondest memories of her, each leaving with a small, framed photograph of a smiling Yevonde.

Self-portrait on a cameo on Junior, 1955.

60 GODDESSES & OTHERS

Self-portrait with daisies, 1930.

Self-portrait in a Tricorne Hat, 1925.

Self-portrait as Harlequin, 1925.

Hon Antonia Pakenham, 1956 (Writer Lady Antonia Fraser).

61
GODDESSES
& OTHERS

62
GODDESSES
& OTHERS

Yevonde wrapped a camera cloth round Annigoni's head to make him look like a wicked old monk. Solarized, 1961.

Model and Mask, 1937.

63
GODDESSES
& OTHERS

64
GODDESSES
& OTHERS

Patricia Rawlings and white dove; solarized portrait, 1961.

Emperor Haile Selassie, Addis Ababa, 1964.

65
GODDESSES
& OTHERS

66
GODDESSES
& OTHERS

Cecil Beaton, 1968. He returned this with 'Too much like last year's turkey' on the back.

Kathy Biggar by Mrs Middleton, 1969.

67
GODDESSES
& OTHERS

68
GODDESSES
& OTHERS

Machine worker in summer, 1937.

Thor Heyerdahl working on American Indians in the Pacific, 1952

69
GODDESSES
& OTHERS

Bibliography

Madame Yevonde's autobiography *In Camera* was published by John Gifford in 1940. During the late 1960s she wrote a set of memoir-notes relating the main events of her life and career under the title *Ten Thousand Sitters*, which remained unfinished and unpublished.

David Mellor's critique in the Arts Council catalogue, *Modern British Photography 1919–1939* published in 1980, set Yevonde in context. Her work is discussed in Val Williams' book *Women Photographers – The Other Observers 1900 to the present* published in 1986 by Virago, and in an article by Val Williams for *The Photographic Collector*, Vol IV, No.2, Autumn 1983.

Kathy Biggar wrote about Yevonde's career in *The Photographic Journal* of June 1973 and Ronald Callender published an article in *The Photographer* for June/July 1973 to coincide with the exhibition of Yevonde's life work at the Royal Photographic Society. Ronald Callender also dealt with the Vivex process in relation to Madame Yevonde's colour work in a series a features entitled *Viva Vivex* in *The Photographer* of January, February, and March of 1978. Tessa Codrington wrote a personal account of Yevonde in *Image* magazine of October 1984 and Ronald Callender's essay *Madame Yevonde's World* was published in the *The British Journal of Photography* January 21st 1988.

Exhibitions

Photographs by Yevonde, 1932, The Albany Gallery, Sackville Street, London W1.
An Intimate Exhibition – Goddesses and Others, 1935, 28, Berkeley Square, London W1.
The Queen Mary, 1936, 28, Berkeley Square, London W1.
Children of Bedford Gardens, 1955, 16a Trevor Street, London SW7.
Dove or Predator?, 1961, 16a Trevor Street, London SW7.
Ethiopia, 1965, 16a Trevor Street, London SW7.
Distinguished Women, 1968, 16a Trevor Street, London SW7.
Sixty Years a Portrait Photographer, 1973, Royal Photographic Society, London WC2.
Madame Yevonde – Colour, Fantasy and Myth, R.P.S., Bath and National Portrait Gallery, London, 1990.

Kate Salway

Kate Salway is an artist and photographer. Having read Fine Art at the University of Reading and at the Slade School, she was art historian at Kingston Polytechnic for a number of years before working as a portrait photographer in New York from 1977–80. She has written extensively for *The British Journal of Photography* and *Photography* magazine since 1980 as well as contributing portrait photographs to *Creative Review* and many other books and magazines. Her colour photographs have been exhibited internationally, published in books and journals and bought for public and private collections in this country and abroad. She lives in London with her husband and son.

Photograph By PETER ESPE

Index

Abdy, Lady Diana colour pages
Adams, Marcus 19,30
Adamson, Joy 57
Addis Ababa 56,57
Albany Gallery 29
Andromeda colour pages
Annigoni 54, 62
Apollon Musagete 15
Arethusa 44 & colour pages
Ariel colour pages
Astor, Nancy Lady 57

Baddeley, Hermione 15
Balcon, Lady Michael colour pages
Ball, Colonel Jack 16
Ballets Russes 15
Basil, Mrs Angus 17
Bayley, Mrs Wansey 12
Bear Lane, Farnham 49,50
Beaton, Cecil 54, 58
Beatty, Lady 30
Beck, Hon. Mrs James 42,44
Bedford Gardens 53,55
Bennett, Arnold 15
Berkeley Square 30-32, 43, 48, 53
Bernstein, Ruby 54
Biggar, Kathy 58, 59, 67
Biggart, Margaret 53
Bishop, Molly 57
Bluebird, The 20-22
Bown, Jane 57
British Journal of Photography 17, 43
Broomfield, Maurice 50, 51, 53
Brown, John 32, 34
Business & Professional Women's Association 35
Bystander, The 30, 44

Callender, Ronald 28,58,59
Campbell, Lady Dolly 44
Campbell, Sir Malcolm 1,20,21,22
Campbell, William 1
Cameron, Julia Margaret 18,35
Cartland, Barbara 15
Castle, Barbara 57
Charles, Lallie 4,5,6,9,18
Chaplin, Charlie 23
Churchill, Winston 15
Codrington, Tessa 56
Coleridge, Lady Georgina 53
Connell, Lena 4,17
Collins, Joan 53
Coronation, Elizabeth II 54
         George VI 36
Coward, Noel 15
Cowell, Elizabeth colour pages
Crisis, 1939 47,48
Cumbers, Ethel 1,22
Cumbers, Frederick 1,22
Cumbers, Verena 1
Curzon, Viscountess 14

Daily Express, the 36
Daily Mail, the 15
Dallmeyer lens 9
Daphne 42,55
Daytona Beach 19
Debrett's 56
Dench, Judi 54
Derwent, Lady 30
Deslys, Gaby 7,9,54
Dolphin Square 48
Doubrovska, Felia 15,25
Douglas-Home, Sir Alec 59
Doves and Predators 54

Earhart, Amelia 22
Echlin, Erland 34
Eden, Mrs Anthony 45
Edwards, Swinford 9
Ellis, Mary 37
Ethiopia 56,57
Europa 45 and colour pages
Evans, Edith 15,57

Forshaw, Ann 56,58
Fortune magazine 32,33
Fraser, Lady Antonia 61
Frost, David 59

Gerson, Mark 58
Gielgud, John 52
Gisborne, Dorothy 45
Gisborne, Paula 53,58
Gloucester, Duke and Duchess of 32,36,38
Greene, Evelyn 4
Gregory, Yvonne 17,30

Hampshire, Susan 57
Harris, Richard 53
Harrods 54
Hart-Davis, Mrs Richard colour pages
Hartnell, Norman 32,36,38
Head, Dora 17
Hecate 45
Hepworth, Barbara 57
Heyerdahl, Thor 53,69
Homes and Gardens magazine 54
Hoppe E.O. 9
Howard, Elizabeth Jane 57
Hoyle, Susan 53,58
Hughes, Alice 17,18
Hunt, Martita 15
Hussey, Olivia 57
Huxley, Aldous 15

Ilford 50
Institute of Incorporated Photographers 59

Junior the cat 59

Keighley-Peach, Peter 49
Kendall, Kay 53
Kenney, Annie 2
Kent, Duke of 36,51
Kent, Princess Marina of 36,51,57

Kent, Princess Alexandra of 3,6,51
Kent, Prince Edward of 36,51
Kodak 54 30 56
Knight, Dame Laura 57

Lambert, Mrs Constant 26
Lambert, Herbert 19
Lane, Sir Allen 16
Lane, Judge Elizabeth 57
Lawrence, Gertrude 45
Leigh, Vivien 52
Lewis, Sinclair 15
Lifar, Serge 15
Lingholt 1

Man Ray 44,45,54
Marceau, Marcel 54
Marshall, Sylvia 10,54
Maude, Joan 30 and colour pages
Mayer, Mrs Edward 44
McLean, Isobel 39
Medusa 44 and colour pages
Middleton, Edgar 15,16,31,48
Milbanke, Lady 44 and colour pages
Minerva colour pages
Morris, Margaret 13,16
MPP Camera 53,56
Mountbatten, Lord and Lady 36, 57
Movietone News 22,35
Murdoch, Iris 57

National Portrait Gallery 58
Neilson, Marion 17
Nesbitt, Cathleen 15
Newberry, Mary 54
New York 22,32
Night Hawks, the 2
Niobe 44 and colour pages
Northumberland, Duchess of 36,54

Observer, the 59
Oliver, Rosina Muriel 17
Oxland, Myrtle 54

Pankhurst, Christabel 2
Pankhurst, Emmeline 10
Pankhurst Museum 56
Paris 2,35
Park, Bertram 30
Penthesilea 44 and cover
Pestel, Madame 17
Powerscroft Farm 10
Professional Photographers Assn. 15,17
Psyche 45
Puddefoot, Susan 58

Queen Mary, R.M.S. 32,33,34,40, 50

Rawlings, Patricia 64
Reinberg, Mme Genia 17
Repeating back camera 29,33
Rhondas, Willie 50,53

Rhondda, Lady 35
Rhys, Lady Anne 41,43
Robeson, Paul 52
Rolleiflex 53,54,56
Ross, Mrs Donald 45
Ross lens 27
Royal Photographic Society 30,43, 58
Russell, Sir John 56

St. James' Palace 36
St Stephen's hospital 59
Save the Children Fund 54
Schiaparelli, Elsa 35
Scott, Lady Alice 32,38
Scott, Chloe 59
Searle, Ronald 51
Selassie, Haile 56,65
Seyler, Athene 57
Sharp, Evelyn 4
Shawcross, Lady Joan 54
Sichel, Ursula 10
Sitwell, Sacheverell 15
Sketch, the 15,30,36,44
Solarization 54
Sorbonne, the 2
Speaight, Richard 17,19
Spencer, Dr D.A. 27,28
Steibel, Victor 37
Surrealism, International Exhibition of 45
Swathling, Lady 36

Tanqueray, Paul 30
Tatler the 30,43,56
Taylor-Hobson, lens 29
Telegraph, the 56
Temple, the 16
Times the 15,56,58
Trevor Street 54,55
Truman, Christine 57
Tutin, Dorothy 57

Van Damm, Florence 17
Verviers 2
Victoria Street 9,17,19,30
Vincent, Lady Helen 8
Vivex Camera 28,29,33
Vivex Process 27,28

Waldberg, Patrick 45
Waugh, Evelyn 15
Wellington, Duchess of 45
Westminster Gazette, the 16
West, Rebecca 15,52,57
Weymouth, Lady 41
Wilding, Dorothy 17,30
Wollstonecraft, Mary 2
Women's Rotary Club 35
Women's Social and Political Union 2
Wood, Mrs Ken 44,48
Works, the 6
World War I 10,11,15,22
World War II 48,49,50

Zinkeison, Anna 33,34,40
Zinkeison, Doris 33,34